PIANO • VOCAL

Broadway Musicals

Show by Show

1940-1949

2:24

Contents

7777 West Bluemound Road P.O. Box 13819 Milwaukee, WI 53213

ISBN 0-7935-0780-4

Foreword

The Broadway musical, with its combination of music, dancing and visual delights, is truly one of America's great cultural treasures. From the hundreds of productions which have been mounted since 1891, we've selected the best music, and combined it with interesting facts and photographs to create a one-of-a-kind seven-volume songbook series: Broadway Musicals - Show By Show.

About The Author Of The Text

The comments about each show in this collection are excerpted from the book *Broadway Musicals Show by Show* by author Stanley Green. Mr. Green (1923-1990) was highly regarded as one of the leading scholars in the field of musical theatre. His eleven books are among the most widely read on the subject, including *The World of Musical Comedy, The Rodgers and Hammerstein Story, Broadway Musicals of the 30s, Starring Fred Astaire, Encyclopaedia of the Musical Theatre, Encyclopaedia of the Musical Film, The Great Clowns of Broadway, Broadway Musicals Show by Show,* and *Hollywood Musicals Year by Year.* He also compiled and edited *The Rodgers and Hammerstein Fact Book,* the definitive reference on that phenomenally successful collaboration.

Mr. Green was born in New York and lived there throughout his life. He began his writing career as a record reviewer for *Saturday Review,* and later was a contributing editor for *HiFi/Stereo Review.* His articles appeared regularly in such publications as *The New York Times, Musical America, Variety,* and *The Atlantic Monthly.* He worked as a film publicist in New York and London, and was public relations advisor to ASCAP for the years 1961-1965. In 1967 he wrote the script for the revue *Salute to the American Musical Theatre,* first performed at the Waldorf-Astoria, and subsequently presented at the White House on three consecutive evenings. He also wrote the script for "The Music of Kurt Weill" and was music advisor for "Review of Reviews," two programs presented at Lincoln Center in New York.

In 1974, at the request of Richard Rodgers, Mr. Green appeared with the composer on the first videotaped program for the Theatre Collection of the New York Public Library at Lincoln Center. He has been involved with many recording projects, including a 100-record series on Broadway musicals for the Franklin Mint, and the album *Starring Fred Astaire,* which he co-produced for Columbia. In 1987 he moderated a series of seminars marking the 100th birthday of George Abbott. Mr. Green presented many lectures on musical theatre and film at Union College, University of Hartford, New York University, C. W. Post College, Lincoln Center Library, Goodspeed Opera, and Marymount College. He continued to be active as a writer and researcher until the time of his death in December of 1990.

LOUISIANA PURCHASE

Music & lyrics:
Irving Berlin

Book:
Morrie Ryskind & B. G. DeSylva

Producer:
B. G. DeSylva
(Irving Berlin uncredited)

Director:
Edgar MacGregor

Choreographer:
George Balanchine

Cast:
William Gaxton, Vera Zorina, Victor Moore, Irene Bordoni, Carol Bruce, Nick Long Jr., Hugh Martin, Ralph Blane, Edward H. Robins

Songs:
"Louisiana Purchase"; "It's a Lovely Day Tomorrow"; "Outside of That I Love You"; "You're Lonely and I'm Lonely"; "Latins Know How"; "What Chance Have I?"; "The Lord Done Fixed Up My Soul"; "Fools Fall in Love"; "You Can't Brush Me Off"

New York run:
Imperial Theatre, May 28, 1940; 444 p.

Louisiana Purchase. William Gaxton, Vera Zorina, Victor Moore, and Irene Bordoni at the Mardis Gras. (Lucas & Monroe)

After playing a Vice President in *Of Thee I Sing* and *Let 'Em Eat Cake* and an Ambassador in *Leave It to Me!,* Victor Moore endeared himself to audiences again by impersonating a United States Senator in *Louisiana Purchase.* In the libretto, prompted by recent revelations of corruption involving the late political leader Huey Long, the seemingly innocent Senator Oliver P. Loganberry goes to New Orleans to investigate the shady operations of the Louisiana Purchasing Company. Jim Taylor (William Gaxton), the company's president, tries to block the probe by involving the incorruptible Senator first with Marina Van Linden (Vera Zorina), a Viennese refugee, then with Mme. Yvonne Bordelaise (Irene Bordoni), a local restaurateuse. Loganberry manages to get out of the trap by marrying Yvonne, but he is ultimately defeated when, being a politician, he is unwilling to cross the picket line in front of the building in which his hearings are to take place. The second of producer B. G. DeSylva's three hits in a row, *Louisiana Purchase* marked Irving Berlin's return to Broadway after an absence of almost seven years. Moore, Zorina, and Bordoni were joined by Bob Hope for the 1941 movie.

PANAMA HATTIE

Music & lyrics: **Cole Porter**

Book: **Herbert Fields & B. G. DeSylva**

Producer: **B. G. DeSylva**

Director: **Edgar MacGregor**

Choreographer: **Robert Alton**

Cast:
Ethel Merman, Arthur Treacher, James Dunn, Rags Ragland, Pat Harrington, Frank Hyers, Phyllis Brooks, Betty Hutton, Joan Carroll, June Allyson, Lucille Bremer, Vera Ellen, Betsy Blair

Songs:
"My Mother Would Love You"; "I've Still Got My Health"; "Fresh as a Daisy"; "Let's Be Buddies"; "Make It Another Old-Fashioned, Please"; "I'm Throwing a Ball Tonight"

New York run:
46th Street Theatre, October 30, 1940; 501 p.

According to Ethel Merman, Hattie Maloney in *Panama Hattie* was an expansion of the Katie who went to Haiti in *DuBarry Was a Lady.* The show was the first in which Miss Merman received solo star billing and it had the longest run of the five musicals in which she was spotlighted singing the songs of Cole Porter. Ethel's Hattie is a brassy, gold-hearted nightclub owner in Panama City who becomes engaged to divorcé Nick Bullitt (James Dunn), a Philadelphia Main Liner. In order for the couple to marry, however, Hattie must first win the approval of Nick's snotty eight-year-old daughter (Joan Carroll), which she accomplishes through the conciliatory "Let's Be Buddies." *Panama Hattie* was the last of the three-in-a-row hits produced by B. G. DeSylva. In 1942, a movie version co-starred Ann Sothern and Red Skelton.

PAL JOEY

Music:
Richard Rodgers

Lyrics:
Lorenz Hart

Book:
John O'Hara (George Abbott uncredited)

Producer-director:
George Abbott

Choreographer:
Robert Alton

Cast:
Vivienne Segal, Gene Kelly, June Havoc, Jack Durant, Leila Ernst, Jean Casto, Van Johnson, Stanley Donen, Tilda Getze

Songs:
"You Mustn't Kick It Around"; "I Could Write a Book"; "That Terrific Rainbow"; "Happy Hunting Horn"; "Bewitched"; "The Flower Garden of My Heart"; "Zip"; "Den of Iniquity"; "Take Him"

New York run:
Ethel Barrymore Theatre, December 25, 1940; 374 p.

Pal Joey. Gene Kelly, June Havoc, and Jack Durant. (Fred Fehl)

With its heel for a hero, its smoky nightclub ambiance, and its true-to-life, untrue-to-anyone characters, *Pal Joey* was a major breakthrough in bringing about a more adult form of musical theatre. The idea originated with author John O'Hara who suggested to Rodgers and Hart that they collaborate on a musical treatment of O'Hara's series of *New Yorker* short stories about Joey Evans, a small-time Chicago entertainer. In the libretto (written with an uncredited assist from producer-director George Abbott), Joey gets a job at Mike's Club where he is attracted to Linda English (Leila Ernst) but drops her in favor of the rich, bewitched dowager, Vera Simpson (Vivienne Segal). Vera builds a glittering nightclub, the Chez Joey, for her paramour, but she soon tires of him, and at the end — after an encounter with blackmailers Ludlow Lowell (Jack Durant) and Gladys Bumps (June Havoc) — Joey is off in search of other conquests. *Pal Joey* marked the only Broadway musical in which Gene Kelly played a major role.

Though it was well received, the musical had to wait until a 1952 revival to be fully appreciated. Miss Segal repeated her original role and Harold Lang played Joey. During the run Helen Gallagher was succeeded by Nancy Walker as Gladys. In 1976, *Pal Joey* returned to Broadway for two months with Joan Copeland and Christopher Chadman. The 1957 screen version featured Frank Sinatra, Rita Hayworth, and Kim Novak.

Best Foot Forward

Music & lyrics:
Hugh Martin & Ralph Blane

Book:
John Cecil Holm

Producer:
George Abbott (Richard Rodgers uncredited)

Director:
George Abbott

Choreographer:
Gene Kelly

Cast:
Rosemary Lane, Marty May, Gil Stratton Jr., Maureen Cannon, Nancy Walker, June Allyson, Kenny Bowers, Victoria Schools, Tommy Dix, Danny Daniels

Songs:
"The Three B's"; "Buckle Down, Winsocki"; "Just a Little Joint With a Jukebox"; "What Do You Think I Am?"; "Ev'ry Time"; "Shady Lady Bird"

New York run:
Ethel Barrymore Theatre, October 1, 1941; 326 p.

Best Foot Forward. June Allyson, Victoria Schools, and Nancy Walker singing "The Three B's." (Vandamm)

Taking place at Winsocki, a Pennsylvania prep school, *Best Foot Forward* is all about the complications that result from the arrival of Hollywood glamour girl Gale Joy (Rosemary Lane) who, as a publicity stunt, has accepted the invitation of Bud Hooper (Gil Stratton Jr.) to be his date at the annual prom. Not only does this provoke hurt feelings on the part of Bud's steady girl, Helen Schlessinger (Maureen Cannon), it also results in a near-riot when souvenir hungry promtrotters strip the movie star down to her essentials. (John Cecil Holm's libretto was based on his own experience when, as a student at the Perkiomen School near Philadelphia, he had invited movie star Betty Compson to be his prom date. The story he wrote was his idea of what might have happened had she shown up.) The rousing "Buckle Down, Winsocki" became the best-known song in the show, which was the first to present Nancy Walker and June Allyson in major roles. In 1963, an Off-Broadway revival performed a similar function for 17-year old Liza Minnelli and Christopher (then Ronald) Walken. The 1943 screen version featured Lucille Ball, and Misses Walker and Allyson.

Lady In The Dark

Music:
Kurt Weill

Lyrics:
Ira Gershwin

Book:
Moss Hart

Producer:
Sam H. Harris

Directors:
Hassard Short, Moss Hart

Choreographer:
Albertina Rasch

Cast:
Gertrude Lawrence, Victor Mature, Danny Kaye, Macdonald Carey, Bert Lytell, Evelyn Wyckoff, Margaret Dale, Ron Field

Songs:
"One Life to Live";
"Girl of the Moment";
"This Is New";
"The Princess of Pure Delight";
"My Ship";
"Jenny";
"Tschaikowsky"

New York run:
Alvin Theatre, January 23, 1941; 467 p.

Lady in the Dark. Margaret Dale, Danny Kaye, and Gertrude Lawrence. (Vandamm)

Though he originally conceived it as a vehicle for Katharine Cornell, Moss Hart turned *Lady in the Dark* into a vehicle for Gertrude Lawrence by enlisting the services of Kurt Weill and Ira Gershwin and changing it from a play to a musical. The work is concerned with *Allure* magazine editor Liza Elliott, whose inability to make up her mind has led her to seek psychiatric help. This feeling of insecurity contributes to her doubts about marrying her lover, publisher Kendall Nesbitt (Bert Lytell), and makes her think she is falling in love with movie star Randy Curtis (Victor Mature). In the end, however, she realizes that the man who can cure her neuroses is really Charley Johnson (Macdonald Carey), the magazine's cynical advertising manager. How does she know? Charley can complete the song "My Ship," which Liza had learned as a child but is now unable to finish. ("Ah! Sweet Mystery of Life" had served a similar function in *Naughty Marietta.)* All other musical pieces in *Lady in the Dark* — including the tongue-twisting "Tschaikowsky" for Danny Kaye and the raucous showstopper "Jenny" for Miss Lawrence, both part of the colorful circus scene — are performed within the dreams that Liza reveals to her doctor.

Lady in the Dark closed for vacation in June 1941, then reopened in September with Lytell replaced by Paul McGrath, Mature by Willard Parker, Carey by Walter Coy, and Kaye by Eric Brotherson. Following a tour, the musical returned to Broadway in February 1943 and remained for 83 performances. Ginger Rogers and Ray Milland were in the 1944 movie version.

BY JUPITER

Music:
Richard Rodgers

Lyrics:
Lorenz Hart

Book:
Richard Rodgers & Lorenz Hart

Producers:
Dwight Deere Wiman & Richard Rodgers

Director:
Joshua Logan

Choreographer:
Robert Alton

Cast:
Ray Bolger, Constance Moore, Benay Venuta, Ronald Graham, Bertha Belmore, Ralph Dumke, Vera Ellen, Margaret Bannerman

Songs:
"Jupiter Forbid"; "Life With Father"; "Nobody's Heart"; "Ev'rything I've Got"; "Careless Rhapsody"; "Wait Till You See Her"

New York run:
Shubert Theatre, June 3, 1942; 427 p.

By Jupiter. Ray Bolger and Bertha Belmore singing "Life With Father." (Vandamm)

Because of its ancient Greek characters and its Asia Minor setting, *By Jupiter* was something of a successor to the previous Rodgers and Hart hit, *The Boys from Syracuse.* The new work, which tried out in Boston under the title *All's Fair,* was based on the 1932 play, *The Warrior's Husband,* in which Katharine Hepburn had first attracted notice. The musical deals with the conflict between the Greeks and the legendary female warriors called Amazons, who live in a gynarchic land ruled by Queen Hippolyta (Benay Venuta). As one of his 12 labors, Hercules (Ralph Dumke) arrives with a Greek army led by Theseus (Ronald Graham) to steal the queen's magical girdle of Diana, the source of her strength. But when Hippolyta's sister Antiope (Constance Moore) takes one look at Theseus, she soon lays down her spear for love, a gesture her sister warriors only too willingly emulate. During the run, Miss Moore was succeeded by Nanette Fabray.

By Jupiter, which remained the longest on Broadway of any Rodgers and Hart musical during the team's partnership, was the last original show they wrote together. It could have stayed longer had not Ray Bolger (in his first starring role as Sapiens, the queen's husband) quit the cast to entertain American troops in the Far East. One curious aspect of the show's score is that "Wait Till You See Her," its best-known song, was dropped a month after the Broadway opening. In 1967, an Off-Broadway revival of *By Jupiter* ran for 118 performances.

OKLAHOMA!

Music:
Richard Rodgers

Lyrics & book:
Oscar Hammerstein II

Producer:
Theatre Guild

Director:
Rouben Mamoulian

Choreographer:
Agnes de Mille

Cast:
**Betty Garde,
Alfred Drake,
Joan Roberts,
Joseph Buloff,
Celeste Holm,
Howard Da Silva,
Lee Dixon,
Joan McCracken,
Bambi Linn,
George S. Irving,
George Church,
Ralph Riggs,
Marc Platt,
Katharine Sergava**

Songs:
**"Oh, What a Beautiful Mornin'";
"The Surrey With the Fringe on Top";
"Kansas City";
"I Cain't Say No";
"Many a New Day";
"People Will Say We're In Love";
"Pore Jud";
"Out of My Dreams";
"The Farmer and the Cowman";
"All er Nothin'";
"Oklahoma"**

New York run:
St. James Theatre, March 31, 1943; 2,212 p.

Oklahoma! Joan Roberts singing "Many a New Day."

A recognized landmark in the evolution of the American musical theatre, *Oklahoma!* was the initial collaboration between Richard Rodgers and Oscar Hammerstein 11 (in all, they wrote nine Broadway shows together). Under the direction of Rouben Mamoulian and with choreography by Agnes de Mille (her first of 15 book musicals), the production not only fused story, songs, and dances, but introduced the dream ballet to reveal hidden fears and desires of the principal characters. In addition, the musical continued in the paths of *Show Boat* (written by Hammerstein) and *Porgy and Bess* (directed by Mamoulian) by further expanding Broadway's horizons in its depiction of the pioneering men and woman who had once tilled the land and tended the cattle of the American Southwest.

Based on Lynn Riggs' 1931 play *Green Grow the Lilacs, Oklahoma!* is set in Indian Territory soon after the turn of the century. The simple tale is mostly concerned with whether the decent Curly McLain (Alfred Drake) or the menacing Jud Fry (Howard Da Silva) will take Laurey Williams (Joan Roberts) to the box social. Though in a fit of pique, Laurey chooses Jud, she really loves Curly and they soon make plans to marry. At their wedding, there is a joyous celebration of Oklahoma's impending statehood, Jud is accidently killed in a fight with Curly, and the newlyweds prepare to ride off in their surrey with the fringe on top. A comic secondary

Oklahoma! Celeste Holm and Lee Dixon.

Oklahoma! Howard Da Silva and Alfred Drake singing "Pore Jud." (Vandamm)

plot has to do with a romantic triangle involving man-crazy Ado Annie Carnes (Celeste Holm), cowboy Will Parker (Lee Dixon), and peddler Ali Hakim (Joseph Buloff).

After trying out under the title *Away We Go!,* the show was renamed *Oklahoma!* for its Broadway engagement at the St. James Theatre (formerly Erlanger's). It remained there five years nine months, thereby setting a long-run record for musicals that it held until overtaken by *My Fair Lady* 15 years later. Among actors who replaced original-cast members were Howard Keel (Curly), Mary Hatcher (Laurey), and Shelley Winters (Ado Annie). A National Company toured for over a decade, including a return visit to New York that lasted 100 performances. The first road company was headed by Harry Stockwell (Curly), Evelyn Wyckoff (Laurey), Pamela Britton (Ado Annie), and David Burns (Ali Hakim). Those who subsequently toured included John Raitt (Curly), Florence Henderson (Laurey), and Barbara Cook (Ado Annie).

In 1969, the Music Theatre of Lincoln Center mounted a revival with Bruce Yarnell (Curly), Leigh Beery (Laurey), April Shawhan (Ado Annie), Margaret Hamilton (Aunt Eller), and Lee Roy Reams (Will). Ten years later, a new production directed by William Hammerstein (Oscar's son) returned to New York for eight months as part of a two-and-a-half year tour. The 1955 movie version, the first film in Todd-AO, featured Gordon MacRae and Shirley Jones in the leading roles.

CARMEN JONES

Music:
Georges Bizet

Lyrics & book:
Oscar Hammerstein II

Producer:
Billy Rose

Directors:
Hassard Short, Charles Friedman

Choreographer:
Eugene Loring

Cast:
Muriel Smith (or Inez Matthews), Luther Saxon, Carlotta Franzell, Glenn Bryant, June Hawkins, Cosy Cole

Songs:
"Dat's Love"; "You Talk Just Like My Maw"; "Dere's a Café on de Corner"; "Beat Out dat Rhythm on a Drum"; "Stan' Up and Fight"; "Whizzin' Away Along de Track"; "Dis Flower"; "My Joe"

New York run:
Broadway Theatre, December 2, 1943; 502 p.

Adapting his libretto from Meilhac and Halevy's for the 1875 premiere production of *Carmen,* and adhering as closely as possible to the original form, Oscar Hammerstein II set his idiomatic lyrics to Georges Bizet's music and updated the story to World War II. Now Carmen is a worker in a parachute factory in the South (rather than a cigarette factory in Seville), Joe (Don José) is an army corporal who falls in love with the temptress, Cindy Lou (Micaela) is the country girl who loves Joe, and Husky Miller is the boxer (replacing Escamillo the bull fighter) who wins Carmen away from Joe. As did the original, the work ends in tragedy as Joe stabs Carmen to death outside a sports stadium while the crowd can be heard cheering Husky. In addition to the staging, Hassard Short was also responsible for the striking color schemes used throughout the production. *Carmen Jones* returned twice to New York during its year-and-a-half nationwide tour. The 1954 film adaptation featured Dorothy Dandridge, Harry Belafonte, and Diahann Carroll.

ONE TOUCH OF VENUS

Music:
Kurt Weill

Lyrics:
Ogden Nash

Book:
S. J. Perelman & Ogden Nash

Producer:
Cheryl Crawford

Director:
Elia Kazan

Choreographer:
Agnes de Mille

Cast:
**Mary Martin,
Kenny Baker,
John Boles,
Paula Laurence,
Teddy Hart,
Ruth Bond,
Sono Osato,
Harry Clark,
Allyn Ann McLerie,
Helen Raymond,
Lou Wills Jr.,
Pearl Lang**

Songs:
**"One Touch of Venus";
"How Much I Love You";
"I'm a Stranger Here Myself";
"West Wind";
"Foolish Heart";
"The Trouble With Women";
"Speak Low";
"That's Him";
"Wooden Wedding"**

New York run:
Imperial Theatre, October 7, 1943; 567 p.

One Touch of Venus. Barber Kenny Baker slipping the ring on statue Mary Martin's finger. (Vandamm)

One Touch of Venus combined the music of composer Kurt Weill (it was his most lighthearted score) with the libretto of two celebrated humorists, poet Ogden Nash and short-story writer S.J. Perelman (it was their only Broadway book musical). In her first starring role, Mary Martin played a statue of Venus recently unveiled in a New York museum, the Whitelaw Savory Foundation of Modern Art, that comes to life after barber Rodney Hatch (Kenny Baker) places a ring on the statue's finger. There is much comic confusion when Savory (John Boles) falls in love with Venus and Venus falls in love with Rodney, but after dreaming of her humdrum life as a barber's wife in Ozone Heights, the goddess happily turns back to marble. Fortunately, Rodney meets a girl who looks just like the statue (Miss Martin, of course) who just loves living in Ozone Heights.

Though *One Touch of Venus* (whose hit song was the torchy "Speak Low") was a fantasy in the modern sophisticated vein of Rodgers and Hart's *I Married an Angel,* its origin was a short novel, *The Tinted Venus,* written in 1885 by the English author F. Anstey (né Thomas Anstey Guthrie) who had based his story on the Pygmalion myth. The musical's first draft, by Bella Spewack, suggested Marlene Dietrich for the role of Venus, but when the actress turned down the part the concept was changed from worldly exotic to youthfully innocent after Perelman and Nash replaced Spewack and Mary Martin replaced Dietrich. The movie version, released in 1948, starred Ava Gardner, Robert Walker, and Dick Haymes.

SONG OF NORWAY

Music & lyrics:
Robert Wright & George Forrest based on Edvard Grieg

Book:
Milton Lazarus

Producer:
Edwin Lester

Directors:
Edwin Lester, Charles K. Freeman

Choreographer:
George Balanchine

Cast:
Irra Petina, Lawrence Brooks, Robert Shafer, Helena Bliss, Sig Arno, Alexandra Danilova, Maria Tallchief, Ruthanna Boris

Songs:
"The Legend"; "Hill of Dreams"; "Freddy and His Fiddle"; "Now!"; "Strange Music"; "Midsummer's Eve"; "Three Loves"; "I Love You"; "Piano Concerto in A Minor" (instrumental)

New York run:
Imperial Theatre, August 21, 1944; 860 p.

Song of Norway had its premiere a continent away from Broadway in July 1944, when it was presented by Edwin Lester's Los Angeles and San Francisco Civic Light Opera Association. Following in the tradition of *Blossom Time,* it offered a score based on themes by a classical composer combined with a biographical plot unencumbered by too much fidelity to historical accuracy. Here we have a romanticized tale of the early years of Edvard Grieg (Lawrence Brooks) who, with his friend, poet Rikard Nordraak (Robert Shafer), is anxious to bring new artistic glory to their beloved Norway. Though temporarily distracted from this noble aim by a dalliance in Rome with a flirtatious (and fictitious) Italian prima donna (Irra Petina), Grieg is so affected by the news of Nordraak's death that he returns home to his indulgent wife (Helena Bliss). Suitably inspired after singing a reprise of their love duet, "Strange Music," the composer creates the A-Minor Piano Concerto. *Song of Norway* which was presented by the New York City Opera in 1981 was filmed in 1970 with Tauralv Maurstad and Florence Henderson.

ON THE TOWN

Music:
Leonard Bernstein

Lyrics & book:
Betty Comden & Adolph Green

Producers:
Oliver Smith & Paul Feigay

Director:
George Abbott

Choreographer:
Jerome Robbins

Cast:
Sono Osato, Nancy Walker, Betty Comden, Adolph Green, John Battles, Cris Alexander, Alice Pearce, Allyn Ann McLerie

Songs:
"New York, New York"; "Come Up to My Place"; "I Get Carried Away"; "Lonely Town"; "Lucky to Be Me"; "Ya Got Me"; "Some Other Time"

New York run:
Adelphi Theatre, December 28, 1944; 463 p.

On the Town heralded the Broadway arrival of four major talents — composer Leonard Bernstein, writing partners Betty Comden and Adolph Green, and choreographer Jerome Robbins. Based on the Robbins-Bernstein ballet, *Fancy Free,* the musical expanded the work into a carefree tour of New York City, where three sailors — played by John Battles, Adolph Green, and Cris Alexander — become involved with three girls — Sono Osato, Betty Comden, and Nancy Walker — on a 24-hour shore leave. One of the sailors (Battles) becomes so smitten by the current winner of the subway's "Miss Turnstiles" competition (Miss Osato) that he and his buddies pursue her through the Museum of Natural History, Central Park, Times Square, and Coney Island. The Adelphi Theatre was once located on 54th Street east of 7th Avenue.

There have been two New York revivals of *On the Town.* Joe Layton staged an Off-Broadway version in 1959, with Harold Lang, Wisa D'Orso, and Pat Carroll, and Ron Field staged a Broadway version in 1971 with Ron Husmann, Donna McKechnie, Bernadette Peters, and Phyllis Newman. The movie adaptation, released in 1949, co-starred Gene Kelly, Vera-Ellen, Frank Sinatra, and Betty Garrett.

Bloomer Girl

Music:
Harold Arlen

Lyrics:
E. Y. Harburg

Book:
Sig Herzig & Fred Saidy

Producers:
John C. Wilson & Nat Goldstone

Directors:
E. Y. Harburg, William Schorr

Choreographer:
Agnes de Mille

Cast:
Celeste Holm, David Brooks, Dooley Wilson, Joan McCracken, Richard Huey, Margaret Douglass, Mabel Taliaferro, Matt Briggs, Herbert Ross

Songs:
"When the Boys Come Home";
"Evelina";
"It Was Good Enough for Grandma";
"The Eagle and Me";
"Right as the Rain";
"T'morra, T'morra";
"Sunday in Cicero Falls";
"I Got a Song"

New York run:
Shubert Theatre, October 5, 1944; 654 p.

Bloomer Girl. Joan McCracken showing off her bloomers to Celeste Holm and Margaret Douglass. (Vandamm)

Continuing the Americana spirit of *Oklahoma!, Bloomer Girl* was not only concerned with the introduction of bloomers during the Civil War, it also covered various aspects of the women's reform movement and the struggle for civil rights. The action occurs in Cicero Falls, New York, in 1861, and covers the rebellion of Evelina Applegate (Celeste Holm) against her tyrannical father, a manufacturer of hoopskirts, who wants her to marry one of his salesmen. Evelina is so provoked that she joins her aunt, Amelia "Dolly" Bloomer (Margaret Douglass), in both her crusade for more practical clothing for women and in her abolitionist activities. Evelina's convictions, however, do not prevent her from singing the romantic duet, "Right as the Rain," with Jefferson Calhoun (David Brooks), a visiting Southern slaveholder, who is eventually won over to her cause. *Bloomer Girl* made a star of Celeste Holm (who was succeeded in her role by Nanette Fabray), and it was also noted for Agnes de Mille's "Civil War Ballet," depicting the anguish felt by women who must remain at home while their men are off fighting. The musical returned to New York for six weeks early in 1947.

Broadway has also seen the following Civil War musicals: *The Girl from Dixie* (1903), *Caroline* (1923), *My Maryland* (1927), *My Darlin' Aida* (1952), *Maggie Flynn* (1968), and *Shenandoah* (1 975).

Carousel

Music:
Richard Rodgers

Lyrics & book:
Oscar Hammerstein II

Producer:
Theatre Guild

Director:
Rouben Mamoulian

Choreographer:
Agnes de Mille

Cast:
**John Raitt,
Jan Clayton,
Murvyn Vye,
Jean Darling,
Christine Johnson,
Eric Mattson,
Bambi Linn,
Peter Birch,
Pearl Lang**

Songs:
**"Carousel Waltz" (instrumental);
"You're a Queer One, Julie Jordan";
"Mr. Snow";
"If I Loved You";
"Blow High, Blow Low";
"June Is Bustin' Out All Over";
"When the Children Are Asleep";
"Soliloquy";
"What's the Use of Wond'rin?";
"You'll Never Walk Alone";
"The Highest Judge of All"**

New York run:
Majestic Theatre, April 19, 1945; 890 p.

Carousel. The opening scene with John Raitt and Jan Clayton. (Vandamm)

With *Carousel,* Rodgers and Hammerstein solidified their position as the dominant creators of musical theatre in the Forties. Reunited for the production with their *Oklahoma!* colleagues, the partners transported Ferenc Molnar's 1921 fantasy *Liliom* from Budapest to a New England fishing village between 1873 and 1888. Billy Bigelow (John Raitt), a swaggering carnival barker, meets Julie Jordan (Jan Clayton), a local factory worker, and — in the soaring duet, "If I Loved You" — they are soon admitting their feelings for each other. After their marriage, Billy learns of his impending fatherhood — with his ambivalent emotions expressed in the "Soliloquy" — and, desperate for money, is killed in an attempted robbery. He is, however, allowed to return to earth to do one good deed. This is accomplished when, unseen by his daughter Louise (Bambi Linn), he shows up at her high school graduation to encourage the lonely girl to have confidence in herself by heeding the words to "You'll Never Walk Alone." For almost two years, *Carousel* at the Majestic Theatre (on 44th Street west of Broadway) played across the street from *Oklahoma!* at the St. James. During the Broadway run (the fifth longest of the decade), Raitt was replaced for a time by Howard Keel. The National Company traveled for one year nine months, ending its tour with a Broadway stand lasting 48 performances. Twenty years after the opening, John Raitt again played Billy Bigelow in a revival presented by the Music Theatre of Lincoln Center. The 1956 film version starred Gordon MacRae and Shirley Jones.

UP IN CENTRAL PARK

Music: **Sigmund Romberg**

Lyrics: **Dorothy Fields**

Book: **Herbert & Dorothy Fields**

Producer: **Michael Todd**

Director: **John Kennedy**

Choreographer: **Helen Tamiris**

Cast:
Wilbur Evans, Maureen Cannon, Betty Bruce, Noah Beery, Maurice Burke, Charles Irwin, Robert Rounseville

Songs:
"Carousel in the Park"; "When You Walk in the Room"; "Close as Pages in a Book"; "The Big Back Yard"; "April Snow"

New York run:
New Century Theatre, January 27, 1945; 504 p.

Celebrated for his lush scores for operettas in exotic locales *(The Desert Song, The New Moon),* Sigmund Romberg joined with lyricist Dorothy Fields to recapture the vintage Currier and Ives charms found up in New York's Central Park in the 1870s. The story, a combination of fact and fiction, deals with the efforts of John Matthews (Wilbur Evans), a *New York Times* reporter, to expose Tammany boss William Marcy Tweed (Noah Beery) and the other grafters who are lining their pockets with funds designated for the building of the park. Romance is supplied when John and Rosie Moore (Maureen Cannon), the daughter of a Tweed crony, vow love everlasting in their ardent duet, "Close as Pages in a Book." Deanna Durbin and Dick Haymes were in the 1948 movie version.

ANNIE GET YOUR GUN

Music & lyrics:
Irving Berlin

Book:
Herbert & Dorothy Fields

Producers:
Richard Rodgers & Oscar Hammerstein II

Director:
Joshua Logan

Choreographer:
Helen Tamiris

Cast:
Ethel Merman, Ray Middleton, Marty May, Kenny Bowers, Lea Penman, Betty Anne Nyman, William O'Neal, Lubov Roudenko, Daniel Nagrin, Harry Belaver, Ellen Hanley

Songs:
"Doin' What Comes Natur'lly"; "The Girl That I Marry"; "You Can't Get a Man With a Gun"; "There's No Business Like Show Business"; "They Say It's Wonderful"; "Moonshine Lullaby"; "My Defenses Are Down"; "I'm an Indian Too'; "I Got Lost in His Arms"; "I Got the Sun in the Morning"; "Anything You Can Do"

New York run:
Imperial Theatre, May 16, 1946; 1,147 p.

Annie Get Your Gun. "There's No Business Like Show Business" sing William O'Neal, Marty May, Ethel Merman, and Ray Middleton. (Vandamm)

Annie Get Your Gun was the first of two shows Irving Berlin wrote for Ethel Merman (the other was *Call Me Madam).* The third longest running musical of the Forties, it was also the biggest Broadway hit of their respective careers. Originally, however, composer Jerome Kern was to have written the songs with lyricist Dorothy Fields (also the co-librettist), but Kern's death as he was about to begin the assignment brought Berlin into the project for both music and lyrics. The idea for the show, the only Rodgers and Hammerstein musical production without a Rodgers and Hammerstein score, is credited to Miss Fields who felt that Ethel Merman as Annie Oakley would be surefire casting.

Though unspecified, the period of the story is the mid-1880s. Annie Oakley, an illiterate hillbilly living near Cincinnati, demonstrates her remarkable marksmanship, and is persuaded — through the convincing claim "There's No Business Like Show Business"— to join Col. Buffalo Bill's travelling Wild West Show. Annie, who needs only one look to fall hopelessly in love with Frank Butler (Ray Middleton), the show's featured shooting ace, soon eclipses Butler as the main attraction, which doesn't help the cause of romance. She exhibits her skills at such locales as the Minneapolis Fair Grounds (where she hits the targets while riding on a motorcycle) and at Governor's Island, New York, where, in a shooting contest with Frank, she realizes that the only way to win the man is to let him win the match. The National Company's tour, which began in October 1947, lasted for one year seven months with Mary Martin heading the original touring cast. In 1966, Miss Merman recreated the role of Annie Oakley for a production sponsored by the Music Theatre of Lincoln Center. This revival, which also had Bruce Yarnell and Jerry Orbach in the cast, included a new Berlin song, "An Old-Fashioned Wedding." After a brief tour, the show played two months at the Broadway Theatre. Betty Hutton and Howard Keel were in the 1950 screen adaptation.

Cover designed by Lucinda Ballard.

Following *Annie Get Your Gun,* other show business musical biographies have been written about Gypsy Rose Lee (Sandra Church in *Gypsy,* 1959); Edmund Kean (Alfred Drake in *Kean,* 1961); Sophie Tucker (Libi Staiger in *Sophie,* 1963); Laurette Taylor (Mary Martin in *Jennie,* 1963); Fanny Brice (Barbra Streisand in *Funny Girl,* 1964); George M. Cohan (Joel Grey in *George M!,* 1968); the Marx Brothers (Lewis J. Stadlen, Daniel Fortus, Irwin Pearl, and Alvin Kupperman in *Minnie's Boys,* 1970); Mack Sennett and Mabel Normand (Robert Preston and Bernadette Peters in *Mack & Mabel,* 1974); Phineas T. Barnum (Jim Dale in *Barnum,* 1980); Federico Fellini (Raul Julia in *Nine,* 1982); Tallulah Bankhead (Helen Gallagher in *Tallulah,* 1983); Marilyn Monroe (Alyson Reed in *Marilyn,* 1983); Ned Harrigan and Tony Hart (Harry Groener and Mark Hamill in *Harrigan 'n Hart,* 1985); and Ellie Greenfield (Dinah Manoff in *Leader of the Pack,* 1985).

ST. LOUIS WOMAN

Music:
Harold Arlen

Lyrics:
Johnny Mercer

Book:
Arna Bontemps & Countee Cullen

Producer:
Edward Gross

Director:
Rouben Mamoulian

Choreographer:
Charles Walters

Cast:
Harold Nicholas, Fayard Nicholas, Pearl Bailey, Ruby Hill, Rex Ingram, June Hawkins, Juanita Hall, Lorenzo Fuller

Songs:
"Cakewalk Your Lady"; "Come Rain or Come Shine"; "I Had Myself a True Love"; "Legalize My Name"; "Any Place I Hang My Hat Is Home"; "A Woman's Prerogative"; "Ridin' on the Moon"

New York run:
Martin Beck Theatre, March 30, 1946; 113 p.

Though based on Arna Bontemps' novel, *God Sends Sunday, St Louis Woman* seems also to have been a close relative of *Porgy and Bess.* Set in St. Louis in 1898, the musical tells of fickle Della Green (Ruby Hill in a part intended for Lena Horne), who is the woman of tough saloon owner Biglow Brown (Rex Ingram), but who falls for Li'l Augie (Harold Nicholas), a jockey with an incredible winning streak. Before Brown is killed by a discarded girlfriend, he puts a curse on Li'l Augie which ends both the winning streak and Della's affection. The two, however, are reunited for the final reprise of their ardent "Come Rain or Come Shine." In 1959, a revised version of *St Louis Woman,* with other Harold Arlen songs added and now set in New Orleans, was performed in Amsterdam and Paris under the title *Free and Easy.*

Finian's Rainbow

Music:
Burton Lane

Lyrics:
E. Y. Harburg

Book:
E. Y. Harburg & Fred Saidy

Producers:
Lee Sabinson & William Katzell

Director:
Bretaigne Windust

Choreographer:
Michael Kidd

Cast:
Ella Logan, Albert Sharpe, Donald Richards, David Wayne, Anita Alvarez, Robert Pitkin

Songs:
"How Are Things in Glocca Morra?"; "If This Isn't Love"; "Look to the Rainbow"; "Old Devil Moon"; "Something Sort of Grandish"; "Necessity"; "When the Idle Poor Become the Idle Rich"; "When I'm Not Near the Girl I Love"; "That Great Come-and-Get-It Day"

New York run:
46th Street Theatre, January 10, 1947; 725 p.

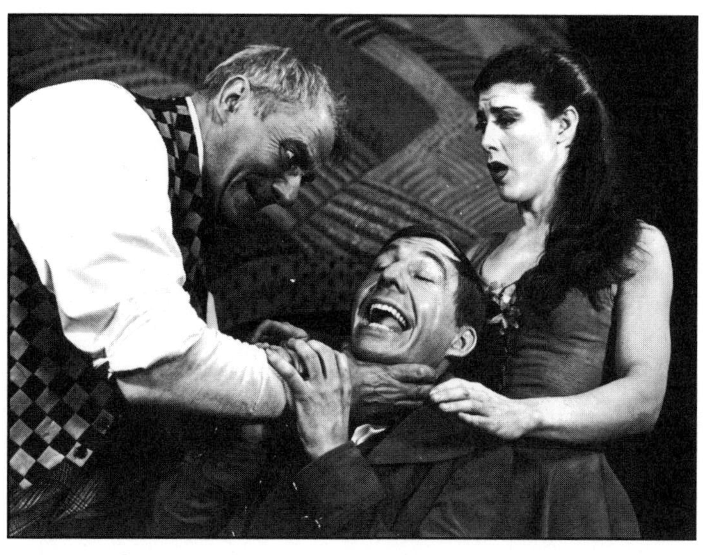

Finian's Rainbow. Albert Sharpe, David Wayne, and Anita Alvarez in a tense moment.

E. Y. Harburg got the idea for *Finian's Rainbow* because he wanted to satirize an economic system that requires gold reserves to be buried at Fort Knox. He then began thinking of leprechauns and their legendary crock of gold that could grant three wishes. In the story that Harburg and Fred Saidy devised, Finian McLonergan (Albert Sharpe), an Irish immigrant, is in Rainbow Valley, Missitucky, to bury a crock of gold which, he is sure, will grow and make him rich. Also part of the fantasy are Og (David Wayne), the leprechaun whose crock has been stolen, Finian's daughter Sharon (Ella Logan), who dreams wistfully of Glocca Morra, Woody Mahoney (Donald Richards), a labor organizer who blames "That Old Devil Moon" for the way he feels about Sharon, and a bigoted Southern Senator, Billboard Rawkins (Robert Pitkin), who — as one of the three wishes — turns black. At the end, everyone comes to understand that riches are found not in gold but in people trusting one another. A 1960 revival had a brief Broadway run. The 1968 movie version starred Fred Astaire, Petula Clark, and Tommy Steele.

High Button Shoes

Music: **Jule Styne**

Lyrics: **Sammy Cahn**

Book: **Stephen Longstreet (George Abbott, Phil Silvers uncredited)**

Producers: **Monte Proser & Joseph Kipness**

Director: **George Abbott**

Choreographer: **Jerome Robbins**

Cast:
Phil Silvers, Nanette Fabray, Jack McCauley, Mark Dawson, Joey Faye, Lois Lee, Sondra Lee, Helen Gallagher, Nathaniel Frey, Johnny Stewart, Paul Godkin

Songs:
"Can't You Just See Yourself?"; "You're My Girl"; "Papa, Won't You Dance With Me?"; "On a Sunday by the Sea"; "I Still Get Jealous"

New York run:
New Century Theatre, October 9, 1947; 727 p.

High Button Shoes, Jule Styne's initial Broadway assignment, offered Phil Silvers his first starring opportunity in the typical role of a brash, bumbling con artist. Though Stephen Longstreet was credited with adapting the story from his own semi-autobiographical novel, *The Sisters Liked Them Handsome,* the musical was completely rewritten by director George Abbott, with an assist from Silvers. In the plot, set in New Brunswick, New Jersey, in 1913, Harrison Floy (Silvers) hoodwinks the Longstreet family into letting him sell some of the valueless property they own. After running off with the profits to Atlantic City (where Jerome Robbins' classic "Keystone Kops" ballet is staged), Floy loses and recovers the money — then loses it forever by betting on the wrong college football team. The musical's showstopper was an old-fashioned song-and-dance polka, "Papa, Won't You Dance With Me?," performed by Nanette Fabray and Jack McCauley.

Allegro

Music: **Richard Rodgers**

Lyrics & book: **Oscar Hammerstein II**

Producer: **Theatre Guild**

Director: **Agnes de Mille (Oscar Hammerstein II uncredited)**

Choreographer: **Agnes de Mille**

Cast:
John Battles, Annamary Dickey, William Ching, John Conte, Muriel O'Malley, Lisa Kirk, Roberta Jonay

Songs:
"A Fellow Needs a Girl"; "You Are Never Away"; "So Far"; "Money Isn't Ev'rything"; "The Gentleman Is a Dope"; "Allegro"

New York run:
Majestic Theatre, October 10, 1947; 315 p.

The third Rodgers and Hammerstein Broadway musical, *Allegro* was their first with a story that had not been based on a previous source. It was a particularly ambitious undertaking, with a theme dealing with the corrupting effect of big institutions on the young and idealistic. The saga is told through the life of a doctor, Joseph Taylor Jr. (John Battles), from his birth in a small midwest American town to his 35th year. We follow Joe's progress as he grows up, goes to school, marries a local belle (Roberta Jonay), joins the staff of a large Chicago hospital that panders to wealthy hypochondriacs, discovers that his wife is unfaithful, and, in the end, returns to his home town with his adoring nurse (Lisa Kirk) to rededicate his life to healing the sick and helping the needy. The show's innovations included a Greek chorus to comment on the action both to the actors and the audience, and the use of multi-level performing areas with nonrepresentational sets.

KISS ME, KATE

Music & lyrics:
Cole Porter

Book:
Samuel & Bella Spewack

Producers:
Saint Subber & Lemuel Ayers

Director:
John C. Wilson

Choreographer:
Hanya Holm

Cast:
Alfred Drake,
Patricia Morison,
Harold Lang,
Lisa Kirk,
Harry Clark,
Jack Diamond,
Annabelle Hill,
Lorenzo Fuller,
Marc Breaux

Songs:
"Another Op'nin', Another Show";
"Why Can't You Behave?";
"Wunderbar";
"So in Love";
"We Open in Venice";
"Tom, Dick or Harry";
"I've Come to Wive It Wealthily in Padua";
"I Hate Men";
"Were Thine That Special Face";
"Too Darn Hot";
"Where Is the Life That Late I Led?";
"Always True to You in My Fashion";
"Bianca";
"Brush Up Your Shakespeare";
"I Am Ashamed That Women Are So Simple"
(lyric: Shakespeare)

New York run:
New Century Theatre,
December 30, 1948; 1,070 p.

Kiss Me, Kate. Alfred Drake taming his shrew Patricia Morison. (Eileen Darby)

After having collaborated ten years earlier on *Leave It to Me!,* Cole Porter and the husband-wife team of Samuel and Bella Spewack were reunited for *Kiss Me, Kate,* the composer's biggest hit and the fourth longest running musical of the Forties. The idea for the show began germinating in 1935 when producer Saint Subber, then a stagehand for the Theatre Guild's production of *The Taming of the Shrew,* became aware that its stars, Alfred Lunt and Lynn Fontanne, quarrelled in private almost as much as did the characters they were portraying in the play. *Kiss Me, Kate* takes place backstage and onstage at Ford's Theatre in Baltimore, from five p.m. to midnight during one day of a tryout of a musical version of *The Taming of the Shrew.* In the plot, egotistical actor-producer Fred Graham (Alfred Drake) and his temperamental co-star and ex-wife, Lili Vanessi (Patricia Morison) fight and make up and eventually demonstrate their enduring affection for each other — just like Shakespeare's Petruchio and Kate. A subplot involves actress Lois Lane (Lisa Kirk) whose romance with actor Bill Calhoun (Harold Lang) is complicated by Bill's weakness for gambling.

Because of the musical's construction, it is possible to follow the story of *The Taming of the Shrew* even though the play-within-the-play is offered only in excerpts. For his lyrics in the musical numbers sung during *The Shrew's* performance, Porter made use of such Shakespearean lines as "I come to wive it wealthily in Padua," "Were thine that special face," "Where is the life that late I led?," and Kate's finale speech beginning "I am ashamed that women are so simple." The more modern sentiments — "Why Can't You Behave?," "So in Love," "Too Darn Hot," and "Always True to You in My Fashion"— were restricted to the theatre's backstage area.

Kiss Me, Kate (the title is from Petruchio's last command in *The Taming of the Shrew)* marked Alfred Drake's first starring part on Broadway and the only major musical in which Patricia Morison originated a leading role. (She won it after it had been rejected by Jarmila Novotna, Mary Martin, Lily Pons, and Jeanette MacDonald.) During the run, Drake was succeeded by Keith Andes and Ted Scott, Miss Morison by Anne Jeffreys, Lisa Kirk by Betty Ann Grove, and Harold Lang by Danny Daniels. The National Company, which toured for one year 11 months, started out with a cast headed by Andes, Jeffreys, Julie Wilson, and Marc Platt, with the first three eventually succeeded by Bob Wright, Frances McCann, and Betty George. In 1953, the Hollywood version put Howard Keel, Kathryn Grayson, Ann Miller, and Tommy Rall in the leads.

LOVE LIFE

Music: **Kurt Weill**

Lyrics & book: **Alan Jay Lerner**

Producer: **Cheryl Crawford**

Director: **Elia Kazan**

Choreographer: **Michael Kidd**

Cast:
Nanette Fabray, Ray Middleton, Johnny Stewart, Cheryl Archer, Jay Marshall

Songs:
"Here I'll Stay"; "Progress"; "I Remember It Well"; "Green-Up Time"; "Economics"; "Mr. Right"

New York run:
46th Street Theatre, October 7, 1948; 252 p.

The only collaboration between Kurt Weill and Alan Jay Lerner, *Love Life* was a highly unconventional work. Billed as "A Vaudeville," it related the story of a non-aging couple (Nanette Fabray and Ray Middleton) and their two children from 1791 to the present, with the theme being the gradual changes in the relationship between people as life in America becomes more complex. The musical pieces were incorporated into the show mostly as commentaries on the characters and situations, in much the same way that Weill had used songs in his early German works. As for the musical's structure, there was no linear plot — with beginning, middle and end — but rather a series of separate but connecting scenes interspersed with vaudeville acts through which the authors conveyed their views. Not quite the format for a long-running smash, perhaps, but the show's innovations did turn up in later productions such as *Company* and *A Chorus Line* (nonlinear stories), *Hallelujah, Baby!* (characters did not age over a long period of time), and *Chicago* (conceived as "A Musical Vaudeville").

WHERE'S CHARLEY?

Music & lyrics:
Frank Loesser

Book:
George Abbott

Producers:
Cy Feuer & Ernest Martin

Director:
George Abbott

Choreographer:
George Balanchine

Cast:
Ray Bolger, Allyn Ann McLerie, Byron Palmer, Doretta Morrow, Horace Cooper, Jane Lawrence, Paul England, Cornell MacNeil

Songs:
"The New Ashmoleon Marching Society and Students' Conservatory Band"; "My Darling, My Darling"; "Make a Miracle"; "Lovelier Than Ever"; "Once in Love With Amy"; "At the Red Rose Cotillion"

New York run:
St. James Theatre, October 11, 1948; 792 p.

Where's Charley? was based on Brandon Thomas's durable 1892 London farce, *Charley's Aunt.* The first Broadway book musical with a score by Frank Loesser (he wrote five shows in all), the musical is concerned with the madcap doings that result when Oxford undergraduates Charley Wykeham (Ray Bolger) and Jack Chesney (Byron Palmer) entertain their proper lady friends, Amy Spettigue (Allyn Ann McLerie) and Kitty Verdun (Doretta Morrow), in their rooms. To do so, Charley must also play chaperon by disguising himself as his own rich aunt "from Brazil where the nuts come from." Transvestite misunderstanding results in complications when the "aunt" must flee the amorous advances of the girls' money-hungry guardian, and when the real aunt makes an unexpected appearance. The show gave Ray Bolger his biggest hit, plus the nightly opportunity to lead the audience in joining him in singing "Once in Love With Amy." Bolger brought the touring company back to Broadway in 1951 for 48 performances, and repeated his part in the 1952 movie version.

South Pacific

Music:
Richard Rodgers

Lyrics:
Oscar Hammerstein II

Book:
Oscar Hammerstein II & Joshua Logan

Producers:
Richard Rodgers & Oscar Hammerstein II, Leland Hayward & Joshua Logan

Director:
Joshua Logan

Cast:
Mary Martin, Ezio Pinza, Myron McCormick, Juanita Hall, William Tabbert, Betta St. John, Martin Wolfson, Harvey Stephens, Richard Eastham, Henry Slate, Fred Sadoff, Archie Savage

Songs:
"A Cockeyed Optimist"; "Some Enchanted Evening"; "Bloody Mary"; "There Is Nothin' Like a Dame"; "Bali Ha'i"; "I'm Gonna Wash That Man Right Outa My Hair"; "A Wonderful Guy"; "Younger Than Springtime"; "Happy Talk"; "Honey Bun"; "You've Got to Be Carefully Taught"; "This Nearly Was Mine"

New York run:
Majestic Theatre, April 7, 1949; 1,925 p.

South Pacific. William Tabbert singing "Younger Than Springtime" to Betta St. John.

The catalyst for the musical was director Joshua Logan who, early in 1948, strongly urged Rodgers and Hammerstein to adapt a short story in James Michener's wartime collection *Tales of the South Pacific* as their next Broadway production. "Fo' Dolla," the story Logan recommended, was about Lt. Joe Cable's tender and tragic romance with a Polynesian girl, but it struck the partners as too close to *Madama Butterfly* to sustain interest throughout an entire evening. Their solution was to make this a secondary plot while using another Michener tale, "Our Heroine," as the main story. That one had to do with the unlikely attraction between Nellie Forbush, a naive Navy nurse from Little Rock, and Emile de Becque, a worldly French planter living on a Pacific island, who fall in love on an enchanted evening. Both stories were combined by having Cable and de Becque go on a dangerous mission together behind Japanese lines, from which only de Becque returns. One of the musical's major themes — expressed through the song "You've Got to Be Carefully Taught" — is the folly of the racial prejudice, an issue that comes up when Emile tells Nellie that he had lived with a native woman who bore him two children.

South Pacific was the first of two musicals (the other was *The Sound of Music)* in which Mary Martin, who played Nellie, was seen as a Rodgers and Hammerstein heroine, and it marked the Broadway debut of Metropolitan Opera basso Ezio Pinza, who played de Becque. It was the second longest running musical of the decade as well as the second musical to be awarded the Pulitzer Prize for drama. Among actors who appeared in the production during its Broadway tenure were Martha Wright and Cloris Leachman (both played Nellie), Ray Middleton (de Becque), Shirley Jones (one of the nurses), Gene Saks (Professor), and Jack Weston (Stewpot).

South Pacific. Mary Martin and Ezio Pinza.

The touring company, which was seen in 118 cities over a period of five years, had a cast originally headed by Janet Blair (Nellie), Richard Eastham (de Becque), Diosa Costello (Bloody Mary), Ray Walston (Luther), Julia Migenes (de Becque's daughter), and Alan Baxter (Comdr. Harbison). Cast replacements on the road included Connie Russell (Nellie), Irene Bordoni (Bloody Mary), and David Burns and Benny Baker (Luther). In 1967, *South Pacific* was revived by the Music Theatre of Lincoln Center with Florence Henderson and Giorgio Tozzi in the leads; 20 years later it was staged by the New York City Opera. The 1958 screen version co-starred Mitzi Gaynor and Rosanno Brazzi (with Tozzi's voice).

MISS LIBERTY

Music & lyrics:
Irving Berlin

Book:
Robert E. Sherwood

Producers:
Irving Berlin, Robert E. Sherwood & Moss Hart

Director:
Moss Hart

Choreographer:
Jerome Robbins

Cast:
Eddie Albert, Allyn Ann McLerie, Mary McCarty, Charles Dingle, Philip Bourneuf, Ethel Griffies, Herbert Berghof, Tommy Rall, Janice Rule, Maria Karnilova, Dody Goodman

Songs:
"Little Fish in a Big Pond"; "Let's Take an Old-Fashioned Walk"; "Home-work"; "Paris Wakes Up and Smiles"; "Only for Americans"; "Just One Way to Say I Love You"; "You Can Have Him"; "Give Me Your Tired, Your Poor" (poem: Emma Lazarus)

New York run:
Imperial Theatre, July 15, 1949; 308 p.

Miss Liberty. Allyn Ann McLerie, Eddie Albert, Mary McCarty, Charles Dingle, Maria Karnilova, and Tommy Rall lead the cast in singing "Give Me Your Tired, Your Poor."

Miss Liberty boasted impressive credentials: songs by Irving Berlin, book by Robert E. Sherwood (his only musical), and direction by Moss Hart. If the results fell somewhat short of expectations, the show was still very much in the Americana mold of *Oklahoma!* and *Bloomer Girl* that offered a comforting view of the past to make audiences feel confident about the future. Here the story — set in New York and Paris in 1885 — deals with the rivalry between two newspapers, the *Herald* and the *World,* and the search for the model who posed for the Statue of Liberty. When the wrong model is brought to New York amid much hoopla, there is the inevitable consternation when the error is discovered. A happy ending is devised, however, just in time for the statue's dedication when all join in singing "Give Me Your Tired, Your Poor."

Gentlemen Prefer Blondes

Music:
Jule Styne

Lyrics:
Leo Robin

Book:
Joseph Stein & Anita Loos

Producers:
Herman Levin & Oliver Smith

Director:
John C. Wilson

Choreographer:
Agnes de Mille

Cast:
Carol Channing, Yvonne Adair, Jack McCauley, Eric Brotherson, Alice Pearce, Rex Evans, Anita Alvarez, George S. Irving, Mort Marshall, Howard Morris, Charles "Honi" Coles, Cholly Atkins

Songs:
"Bye, Bye, Baby"; "A Little Girl from Little Rock"; "Just a Kiss Apart"; "It's Delightful Down in Chile"; "Diamonds Are a Girl's Best Friend"

New York run:
Ziegfeld Theatre, December 8, 1949; 740 p.

Gentlemen Prefer Blondes. Carol Channing singing "Diamonds Are a Girl's Best Friend." (Fred Fehl)

Based on Anita Loos' popular 1926 novel and play of the same name, *Gentlemen Prefer Blondes* took a satirical look at the wild and wacky Twenties, though there was no attempt at parodying the songs and styles as in the manner of Sandy Wilson's *The Boy Friend.* Carol Channing, in her first major role, scored such a success as the gold-digging little girl from Little Rock that she was elevated to stardom during the show's run. The scenes occur mostly aboard the *Ile de France,* which is taking Lorelei Lee and her chum Dorothy Shaw (Yvonne Adair) to Paris, courtesy of Lorelei's generous friend, button tycoon Gus Esmond (Jack McCauley). En route, the girls meet a number of accommodating gentlemen, including Sir Francis Beekman (Rex Evans) who loses a diamond tiara to Lorelei (who thereby wins a best friend) and Henry Spofford (Eric Brotherson), a Philadelphia Main Liner who loses his heart to Dorothy. The 1953 movie version offered Marilyn Monroe and Jane Russell, plus a hybrid score.

In 1973, a new stage version, called *Lorelei,* retained ten songs from the original score and added five new ones by Jule Styne, Betty Comden and Adolph Green. Carol Channing again headed the cast which included Tamara Long (Dorothy), Peter Palmer (Gus), Lee Roy Reams (Henry), and Jack Fletcher (Sir Francis). The book, now credited to Kenny Solms and Gail Parent, retained the same basic story, except for a modern-day prologue and epilogue that found Lorelei reminiscing about the past. After touring 11 months, Lorelei opened on Broadway in January 1974, and gave 320 performances.

It's A Lovely Day Tomorrow

From the Musical Production
"LOUISIANA PURCHASE"

Music and Lyric by
IRVING BERLIN

+) *Symbols for Guitar, Chords for Ukulele and Banjo.*

Bb
Gm7
Cm7
F
Fm7
Bb7
con - so - la - tion in the weath - er re - port
L.H.
CHORUS
(Guitar Tacet)
Eb
Cm7
Ab
Eb
F9
Bb7
Gm
Eb
IT'S A LOVE - LY DAY TO - MOR - ROW, To - mor - row is a
mf-f
Ab
Fm7
Ebdim
Eb
Ab
Eb
love - ly day Come and feast your tear dimmed
Fm7
Bb7
(Guitar Tacet)
Eb
Cm7
Fm
Eb
F7
eyes On to - mor - row's clear blue skies

Bb7
(Guitar Tacet)
Eb
Cm7
Ab
Eb
F9
Bb7
Gm
If to - day your heart is wea - ry, If
Eb
Ab
ev - 'ry lit - tle thing looks gray Just for -
Fm
Fm7
Cdim
Eb
Abm
Eb
Cm7
get your trou-bles and learn to say, TO-MOR-ROW IS A
Fm7
1. Eb
Cdim
Fm7
(Guitar Tacet)
2. Eb
Ab
Eb
LOVE - LY DAY. IT'S A DAY.

MAKE IT ANOTHER OLD FASHIONED, PLEASE

COLE PORTER

Cm G7 Cm F♯7 B♭ F7
feel so much slick - er, Well, that is, most_ of the
B♭sus. 4 B♭ D♭ E♭7 B♭m A♭
time,_ But there are mo - ments, soon - er or lat - er, when it's
Fm7 Guitar tacet A♭ F7 G
tough, I got_ to say, not to say: "Wait - er!_
ten.
ten.
Em G7 Em G7
Subito Slow Rhumba Tempo
f
mf

C
REFRAIN (with much expression)
G7
C
Make it an - oth - er Old Fash - ioned, please,
p-mf
G7 sus. 4
G7
C
C♯dim.
G7
Make it an - oth - er doub - le Old Fash - ioned
C
C7
F
B♭
F
please,
Make it for one who's due To
mf
C
Gm(add6)
A7 sus. 4
A7
Dm
A7
join the dis - il - lus - ioned crew,
Make it for one of love's

Dm
G7
F
B♭m
G7
C
new, ref - u - gees, Once high in my cas - tle,
espr.
p
G7
C
G7 sus. 4
G7
C7
I reigned su - preme, And Oh! what a cas - tle
poco - a - poco
C7
Am7
Dm
E7
built on a heav - en - ly dream, Then
cresc.
D7
E7
A7
Dm
Dm7
quick as a light - ning flash, That cas - tle be - gan to crash, So
mf

C
D7
G7
1. C
G7
make it an-oth-er Old Fash - ioned please!
p
mf
To Coda
2. C
Final ending
C6
C
Coda
G7
please!
please!
Leave out the
mf
p
C
G7
C
G7
cher-ry
Leave out the o-range!
Leave out the
Gm7
A7
D7
Dm7
Dm7(♭5)
C
bit-ters!
Just make it a straight rye!
mf
espr.
f molto cresc.
sf

I COULD WRITE A BOOK

(From "PAL JOEY")

Words by LORENZ HART
Music by RICHARD RODGERS

G Dm7 G7 C G7 C
get, And the sim - ple se - cret of the plot
mf
p
G7 C G7 C C#dim Dm7 G7 F G7
is just to tell them that I love you a lot, Then the
C Ab7 Dm7 G7 Gm7 C7 F Dm C C+
world dis - cov - ers as my book ends, How to make two
Dm7 G7 1 C Dm7 G7 2 C F C
lov - ers of friends. If they friends.
mf
mf

BEWITCHED

(From "PAL JOEY")

Words by LORENZ HART
Music by RICHARD RODGERS

C/E
C+
F6
Fdim
C/E
E♭dim
Dm7
G7
A7-9
sim-per-ing, whim-per-ing child a-gain. Be-witched, both-ered and be-wil-dered am
Dm7
G13
C
Dm7
I.
Could-n't sleep, And would-n't sleep, When
C/E
C+
F6
Fdim
C/E
E♭dim
Dm7
G7
C7-9
love came and told me I should-n't sleep, Be-witched, both-ered and be-wil-dered am
Fmaj7
A7
Dm
Dm(+7)
Dm
I.
Lost my heart, but what of it?

Am
Am(+7)
Am
Dm7
G13
Dm7
G13
He is cold I a - gree, He can laugh, but I love it Al - though the
Em7
Ab7
Dm7
G7-5
G7
C
Dm7
laugh's on me. I'll sing to him, Each spring to him, And
C/E
C+
F6
Fdim
C/E
Ebdim
Dm7
G13
long for the day when I'll cling to him, Be - witched, both - ered and be - wil - dered am
C
Dm7
G13
C
Dm7
C(add9)
I.
I.

Buckle Down, Winsocki

Words and Music by
HUGH MARTIN and RALPH BLANE

sock - i, make 'em yell. You can win, Win - sock - i If you
Gm7 C7 Gm Eb C7
give 'em hell If you don't give in take it
cresc.
Am D7 Gm7 F#dim Gm7
on the chin, You are bound to win, if you will
piu cresc.
C7 F G+ Gm C7
on - ly buck - le down, If you fight you'll chuck - le at de -
Am F6 Db9 C7
feat. If you fight your luck - 'll not re -

F F#dim C7 F6
treat (shout) "we repeat" Knuck - le down Win - sock - i Knuck - le
f mf
down. You can win Win - sock - i, If you
Gm7 C7 Gm Eb C7
buck - le down If you mow them down If you
cresc.
Am D7 Gm7 F#dim Gm7
go to town you can wear the crown if you will
f
1 C7 F 2 C7 F6
on - ly buck - le down. Buck - le on - ly buck - le down.
f

This Is New

(From the Musical Production "LADY IN THE DARK")

Lyrics by IRA GERSHWIN
Music by KURT WEILL

Ebm F♯dim Db6 F♯dim Db6 Ebm
I lost you through the cen-tur-ies. I find you once a-
F7 F7(b5) Bbm C7b5 F7
gain, And find my-self the luck-i-est of men.
Refrain
(slowly, with expression)
Abmaj7 Db7 Abmaj7
This is new, I was mere-ly ex-ist-ing,
p - mf
Bbm7 Ebm
This is new And I'm liv-ing at

F7
Bbm7
Ebm
last,
Head to toe you've
mf
Db6
Ab
Ab7
got me so I'm spell - bound
I don't
3
Dbm
Dbm7
G#dim
Bb7
know if I am heaven or hell - bound.
Guitar Tacet
Abmaj7
Db7
This is new,
is it Ve - nus in -
3
p

Abmaj7
Ab7+
Db
sist - ing,
That I'm through
C7
Fm
C7+
Fm
F7
with the shad-ow - y past?
I am
mf
piu espr.
Bbm
Edim
Eb7
Ab
Fm7b5
hurled Up to an - oth - er world Where life is
Bbm7
Eb+
Eb7
Ab
Dbm
Ab6
bliss And this is new.

My Ship

(From the Musical Production "LADY IN THE DARK")

Lyrics by IRA GERSHWIN
Music by KURT WEILL

Gm7 C7 F D7 G7 C7 F F♯dim
My ship's a - glow with a mil - lion pearls And ru - bies fill each
G7 C+ F D7 Gm A Dm Em
bin, The sun sits high in a sap - phire sky When my ship comes
B♭ F Gm7 Am C7 Gm7 Am C7 Gm7 C7 B♭m
in. I can wait the years Till it ap - pears One fine day one
mp
F E7 Am Dm7 Am Dm7 G7 Edim
spring, But the pearls and such They won't mean much if there's miss - ing just one
mf

G7 C7 F D7 G7 C7
thing. I do not care if that day ar - rives, That
p
F D7 Dm7 C+ F D7 Gm A7
dream need nev - er be, If the ship I sing does-n't al - so bring my
Dm C7 F C7 F Dm Bb7 F Bb
allargando (slower)
own true love to me, If the ship I sing does-n't al - so bring my
mf piu espr.
F Gm Bbm6 C7 F Db7 F
own true love to me.
dim.
p
pp

WAIT TILL YOU SEE HER

(From "BY JUPITER")

Words by LORENZ HART
Music by RICHARD RODGERS

Cm7
G7+ (♭9)
C9 (5♭)
C9
Fm7
B♭7
Pen - sive and sweet and wise.
All of it love - ly,
mp
Cm
Gm
C9
F7 sus6
Fm
All of it thrill - ing; I'll nev - er be will - ing to free
cresc.
mf
G7
E♭m
F7
E7
E♭7
Fm7
her, When you see her, You won't be -
rit.
B♭7 sus6
B♭7
1
E♭
2.
E♭
lieve your eyes.
eyes.
a tempo
rall.

OH, WHAT A BEAUTIFUL MORNIN'

(From "OKLAHOMA!")

Words by OSCAR HAMMERSTEIN II
Music by RICHARD RODGERS

Eb
Bbdim
Bb7
looks like it's climb- in' clear up to the sky.
lit- tle brown mav'- rick is wink- in' her eye.
ol' weep- in' wil- ler is laugh- in' at me!
mf
Eb
Absus
Ab
Eb
Refrain:
Oh, what a beau- ti- ful morn- in', Oh, what a
mp
Bb7
Eb
beau- ti- ful day. I got a beau- ti- ful
Ab
Adim
Eb
Bb7
1,2Eb
Bb7
feel- in' Ev- 'ry- thing's go- in' my way. All the
All the
p
3. Eb
Fm7
Bb7
Eb
Bb7
Eb
way Oh, what a beau- ti- ful day!
ritenuto

THE SURREY WITH THE FRINGE ON TOP

(From "OKLAHOMA!")

Words by OSCAR HAMMERSTEIN II
Music by RICHARD RODGERS

G D7 G D7 G
In the slick - est gig you ev - er see!
G Gmaj7 G6 G Gmaj7 G6 Gmaj7
Chicks and ducks and geese bet - ter scur - ry When I take you out in the sur - rey,
All the world - 'll fly in a flur - ry When I take you out in the sur - rey,
I can see the stars get - tin' blur - ry, When we drive back home in the sur - rey,
G Gmaj7 G6 G Em7 A9 D7
When I take you out in the sur - rey with the fringe on top!
When I take you out in the sur - rey with the fringe on top!
Driv - in' slow - ly home in the sur - rey with the fringe on top!
G Gmaj7 G6 G Gmaj7 G6 Gmaj7
Watch that fringe and see how it flut - ters When I drive them high step - pin' strut - ters.
When we hit that road, hell for leath - er, Cats and dogs 'll dance in the heath - er,
I can feel the day get - tin' old - er, Feel a sleep - y head on my shoul - der

G Gmaj7 G6 G Em7 A9
Nos - ey - pokes 'll peek thru their shut - ters and their eyes will
Birds and frogs 'll sing all to - geth - er and the toads will
Nod - din', droop - in' close to my shoul - der, 'til it falls ker -
Am7 D7 Dm7 G7 C
pop! The wheels are yel - ler, the up - hol - ster - y's brown, The
hop! The wind 'll whis - tle as we rat - tle a - long. The
plop! The sun is swim - min' on the rim of a hill: The
G7 C Em7 A7
dash - board's gen - u - ine leath - er, With is - in - glass cur - tains y' can
cows 'll moo in the clo - ver, The riv - er will rip - ple out a
moon is tak - in' a head - er, And jist as I'm think - in' all the
D Em7 A7 Am7 D7
roll right down, in case there's a change in the weath - er.
whis - pered song, And whis - per it o - ver and o - ver:
earth is still, a lark 'll wake up in the med - der.

G Gmaj7 G6 G Gmaj7
Two bright side - light's wink - in' and blink - in' Ain't no fin - er
Don't you wisht y'd go on for - ev - er? Don't you wisht y'd
Hush, you bird, my ba - by's a - sleep - in' May - be got a
G6 Gmaj7 G Gmaj7 G6 G
rig I'm a - think - in' You c'n keep your rig if you're think - in' 'at I'd
go on for - ev - er? Don't you wisht y'd go on for - ev - er and ud
dream worth a - keep - in' Whoa! you team, and jist keep a - creep - in' at a
Am Bdim Am Bdim Am G Gmaj7 Am7 D7
keer to swap Fer that shin - y lit - tle sur - rey with the fringe on the
nev - er stop In that shin - y lit - tle sur - rey with the fringe on the
slow clip clop. Don't you hur - ry with the sur - rey with the fringe on the
1,2 G F6 D7
top!
top!
3 G C G
top!
mf
f

PEOPLE WILL SAY WE'RE IN LOVE

(From "OKLAHOMA!")

Words by OSCAR HAMMERSTEIN II
Music by RICHARD RODGERS

G7 C
are so like mine Your eyes must-n't
your hand in mine Your hand feels so
mf
p
D9 Dm7 Dm7-5 Dm7 G7 C
glow like mine Peo- ple will say we're in love!
grand in mine Peo- ple will say we're in love!
mf
Cm7 F7 Bb+ Bb Dm6 E7 A7
Don't start col- lect- ing things Give me my rose and my
Don't dance all night with me Till the stars fade from a-
mf
D7 Dm7 Ebdim C Am D7
glove. Sweet- heart they're sus- pect- ing things
-bove, They'll see it's al- right with me
C B C G7 Gdim G7 1. C Am Dm7 2. C
Peo- ple will say we're in love.
Peo- ple will say we're in love.
mf espr.
mf

OKLAHOMA
(From "OKLAHOMA!")

Words by OSCAR HAMMERSTEIN II
Music by RICHARD RODGERS

G7 C F C
O - k - la - hom - a, Ev - 'ry
G7 Gdim G7sus G7 C9
night my hon - ey lamb and I sit a - lone and
F6 Fm6 C G7
talk and watch a hawk mak - in' laz - y cir - cles in the
C F C
sky. We know we be - long to the land

G D7 G9 Em G7
And the land we be - long to is grand! And when we
C D7
(yell)
say Yeeow! A - yip - i - o - ee - ay!
fp
cresc.
G D7 C E7
We're on - ly say - in' You're do - in' fine, Ok - la -
Am Am7 D7 C G7 C
hom - a! Ok - la - hom - a O. K.
sf

SPEAK LOW

(From "ONE TOUCH OF VENUS")

Words by OGDEN NASH
Music by KURT WEILL

G9
C9
C7-9
F6
D7
Gm7
C7
swift, like ships a- drift, we're swept a- part too soon Speak
Gm9
C9
low darling, speak low love is a
spark lost in the dark too soon, too soon, I
Bbm6/9
Eb9
feel wher- ev- er I go that to-mor- row is
F
near, to- mor- row is here and al- ways too soon.

Fm7
Abm
Ebmaj7
Time is so old and love so brief, Love is pure gold and
mf più espressivo
Fdim
E7
C+
Gm9
C9
Gm9
time a thief. We're late dar- ling, we're late
C9
Gm9
C9
Gm9
C7
The cur- tain de- scends, ev- 'ry thing ends too
F6
D
Bbm6/9
Bbm6
soon, too soon I wait dar- ling, I
F
Bb+
D7
G9
C9+5
F
wait Will you speak low to me, speak love to me and soon.
espressivo
rit.
L.H.
p

DAT'S LOVE

Lyrics by **OSCAR HAMMERSTEIN** II / Music by **GEORGES BIZET**
Adapted by Robert Russell Bennett

CARMEN JONES (1943)

Dm A7sus Dm Em7(♭5) Edim7
portamento
stud An' I won' give him a cig - a - rette. One man
taught, An' here's your les - son for to - day: If I
Gm6 Gm A7
treats me like I was mud An' what I got dat — man c'n
chase you, den you'll get caught, But once I got you, I go my
Dm D D7 Bm A7sus D
get. — Dat's love! — Dat's
way! — Dat's love! — dat's
Chorus: Love's a ba - by dat grows up wild An' he don't do - what you want him
If you lis - ten, den you'll get taught, An' here's your les - son for to -

Em7 C/D Em7 Bm
love! Dat's love!
love! Dat's love!
to, Love ain' no - bod - y's an - gel child An' he won'
day: If I chase you, den you'll get caught, But once I
A7/D A7 D A D A D A7
Dat's love! You go for me an' I'm ta - boo, But if yo're
dat's love!
pay an - y mind to you.
got you, I go my way!
D A6 Em6 Bm Em7 Bm Em7 Bm
hard to get, I go for you, An' if I do, den you are through, boy, My

G/D A7 D A D A D A7
baby, dat's de end of you. So take your cue, boy, don'
Chorus: f De end of you! pp
D A7 Em7 Bm Em7 Bm Em7 Bm
say I didn' tell you true. I tol' you truly, If I
Chorus: f She tol' you true. pp cresc.
A7/D D A D A
Chorus
love you, dat's de end of you! You go for me an' I'm ta-
mf mf
D A7 D A Em7 Bm Em7 Bm
boo, But if yore hard to get I go for you, An' if I do, den you are

Em7
Bm7
G/D
A9
D
A
through, boy, My ba - by, dat's de end of you De end of
f
D
p Carmen:
A
D
A7
D
A
you! So take your cue, boy, Don' say I did - n' tell you
p
Em7
Bm
Em7
Bm
Em7
Bm7
A7/D
true. I tol' you tru-ly, If I love you, dat's de end of
f
p
cresc.
f
D
1.
D
2.
you!
you!
ff
f
ff

STRANGE MUSIC

Based on "Nocturne" & "Wedding Day In Troldhaugen" by EDVARD GRIEG
Musical Adaption by ROBERT WRIGHT & GEORGE FORREST

C7
D7
B♭m6
C7
I can hear the chords re - sound of bound - ing brass that seems to say, I've
D♭
B♭7
B♭m7
Gdim
found you! I've found you! I've found
poco rit.
A♭
B♭m7
E♭9
E♭7 (♭9)
you!
calando
Refrain (slowly with expression)
A♭
A♭6
Strange mu - sic in my ears only

A♭dim
B♭m7
E♭7
D♭
now as you spoke, did it start.
Strange
mf
B♭m7
E♭7
mu - sic of the spheres
Could its love - ly hum be
B♭m7
E♭7
A♭
E♭m7
F7
com - ing from my heart?
You ap - pear and I hear
p
mp
B♭m
G7(sus. 4)
G7
F♯7
G7
song sub - lime
Song that I'm in - ca - pa - ble
cresc.

Cm
Bbm7
Eb7
Ab
of.
So
dear,
let
me
hold
you
mf
p
F7(b5)
F7
Bbm7
Eb9
Bbm7
Eb7
near
While
we
treas - ure
ev - 'ry
meas - ure,
so
that
Ab
Eb7
Ab
Ab7
E7
Bbm7
Eb7
time
can
nev - er
change
The
strange,
new
mu - sic
of
cresc.
f
3
1.
Ab
Eb7
2.
Ab
Db9
Ab
love.
love.
3
3
L.H.
ff
Ped.
*

I LOVE YOU

Words and Music adaptation
based on EDWARD GREIG Music
Words by ROBERT WRIGHT and GEORGE FORREST

Dm9
Dm7
Dm7-5
G7
love the tear that dims your danc - ing eyes; I love you dear, and there your
cresc.
ff
rit.
C
G
Dsus
G7
an - swer lies.
mp
a tempo
dim.
C
G
Dm
And should you ask if time has dulled my long - ing,
p a tempo
A7
D9
Am7/D
Say, has the North - ern star gone cours - ing South?
mf

G7
C
G
If me you doubt, 'Tis on - ly you you're
p
Dm
A7
D9
wrong - ing, I loved you then, I love you now, I'll
Dm9
Dm7
Dm7-5
G7
love you when the world grows old and dies; I love you dear, and here your
cresc.
ff rit.
C
G
Dsus
G7
C
an - swer lies.
mp
a tempo
dim.
pp

NEW YORK, NEW YORK
(From "ON THE TOWN")

Words by BETTY COMDEN and ADOLPH GREEN
Music by LEONARD BERNSTEIN

Cm
Ab7
We'll find___ the ro - mance and dan - ger wait - ing
I prom - ised dad - dy I would - n't miss on
There's just___ one thing___ that's im - port - ant in Man-
Eb
Cdim/Bb Bb7
Eb
in it be - neath the Broad - way lights;___ But we've hair___
an - y and we have just one day;___ Got - ta see___
hat - tan when you have just one day;___ Got - ta pick___
Bb7
___ on our chest,___ so what we___ like the best___ are the nights,___
___ the whole town___ right from Yonk - ers on down___ to the bay___
___ up a date,___ may be sev - en or eight___ on your way,___
Eb6
Cdim/Bb Bb7
Eb
___ sights, lights, nights.___ New
___ in just one day.___ New
___ in just one day.___ New

G6
D7
G6
York, New York, a hell - uv - a town, The
York, New York, a vis - i - tor's place, Where
York, New York, a hell - uv - a town, The
D7
G6
Bronx is up but the Bat - ter - y's down, And
no one lives on ac - count of the pace, But
Bronx is up but the Bat - ter - y's down, And
D7
G6
F7
peo - ple ride in a hole in the ground; New
sev - en mil - lion are scream - ing for space; New
peo - ple ride in a hole in the ground; New
1,2
B♭
D7
York, New York, it's a hell - uv - a town!
York, New York, is a vis - i - tor's place!

G
G7
E♭6
B♭m7
E♭6
B♭maj7
B♭m7
B♭
York, New York,
D7
G
it's a hell - uv - a town!
f
ff
C7
G6
E♭
D9
G

EVELINA

(From The Musical Production "Bloomer Girl")

Lyric by E.Y. HARBURG
Music by HAROLD ARLEN

Bbm9
Eb7(9b)
Bbm9
Eb9
Bbm9
Eb9+5
ya gon-na keep de-lay-in' the day.
Cm7
F9
Cm9
F7(9b)
Fm7
Don't ya reck-on it's wrong
Tri-flin' with A-pril this
Bb7+5
Eb
Edim.
way?
E-ve-li-na, won't ya pay a lit-tle mind to me
poco rit
p
a tempo
Fm7
Eb7
Bbdim.
Bb9
G7+5
C7+5
soon?
Wake up!

Bb7+5
Eb6
Eb
G7
Db11+
C7
C7+5
Wake up! The earth is fair, the fruit is fine ___ But
Fm7
Edim.
Eb
D7+5
G9
what's the use o' smel-lin' wa-ter mel-on cling-in' to an-oth-er fel-la's
C7
Fm7
Eb
F9
Fm7
vine? E - ve-li-na, won't ya roll off that vine an' be
(espr.)
poco rit.
1. Eb
Fm7
Bb7
2. Eb
B7
Bb7
Eb
mine?
mine? ___
a tempo mf
rit.
pp

IF I LOVED YOU
(From "CAROUSEL")

Words by OSCAR HAMMERSTEIN II
Music by RICHARD RODGERS

C#7
C/E
F
fraid and shy, I'd let my gold - en chanc - es
Bb
D7/A
Fm/Ab
G7
C
Cdim
pass me by! Soon you'd leave me,
f
mf
C/E
C+/E
F
B7/A
off you would go in the mist of day, Nev - er, nev - er to
C/G
Em/G
F6
Cmaj7/E
Dm7
know How I loved you,
Dm7sus
Dm7
G7
C
F
Dm7
G7-9
Csus
C
If I Loved You. Loved You.
f
rit.
mp
a tempo
mp

June Is Bustin' Out All Over

Bb7 A7 F#m7 B7 Em7 A11 A7 D Em
push - es ev - 'ry lit - tle wheel that wheels be - side a mill!
jeep - ers Out - a all the morn - in'
R.H.
Fdim D7/F# Em7 A7 D Cm/Eb D7
glor - ies on the fence! Be - cause it's
Gmaj7 G6 G Fm6 E7
June! June, June, June,
Am7 E7 Eb7 Tacet Am7 D13
Jest be - cause it's June! June!
ff
Gmaj9 G Ab6/9 Gmaj9
June!

YOU'LL NEVER WALK ALONE
(From "CAROUSEL")

Words by OSCAR HAMMERSTEIN II
Music by RICHARD RODGERS

C7 F Bdim C
mf
Walk on through the wind, Walk on through the
Fm6 C Em F G9 G7
cresc.
rain, Tho' your dreams be tossed and blown Walk
C C+ F D7
poco a poco
on, walk on, with hope in your heart, And you'll
C C+ Fmaj7 F#7-5 Em G7
nev- er walk a- lone, You'll
C C+ F G9 C Em Fmaj7 F F Dm Em C
molto espr.
dim.
mf
rit.
nev- er walk a- lone! When you -lone!
ff
8ba

CLOSE AS PAGES IN A BOOK

(From "UP IN CENTRAL PARK")

Words by DOROTHY FIELDS
Music by SIGMUND ROMBERG

Fm7 Fm6 Ebmaj7 Eb7 Ab F7 Fm7 Bb7+5
And when a tear starts to ap-pear, My eyes grow mist-y too.
Eb Bbm7 Eb7 Ab Eb7 Ab Ab7
Our dreams won't come tumb-ling to the ground, Well hold them fast.
F7 Cm7 F7 Bb F7 Bb7 Gm Eb Gm
Dar-ling, as the strong-est book is bound, We're bound to last. Your life is
G7 G7+5 G7 Cm Ab6 B7 Eb
my life and while life beats a-way in my heart We'll be Close As
Bbm6 C7 Fm7 Bb9+5 Eb Bbdim Bb7 Eb
Pag-es In A Book, Nev-er to part. part.

ANY PLACE I HANG MY HAT IS HOME

(From The Musical Production "St. Louis Woman")

F
F
F
home!
Sweet - nin' wa-ter
8va
mp
f
cher - ry wine,
Thank you kind-ly,
suits me fine
loco
8va
loco
B♭
F
F+
D♭
B♭m6
F
Kan - sas Ci - ty,
Ca - ro - line,
That's my hon - ey - comb
8va
loco
B♭7
F
Gm
Fdim
Gm
F
A♭
G
G♭
Fm
'Cause an - y place I hang my hat is home.

Fm
D♭
B♭7
E♭
C7
Birds roost-in' in the tree pick up an' go An' the go-in' proves
mf rhythmically, with expression
Fm
B♭7
D7
A♭m
C7
That's how it ought to be, I pick up too When the spir-it moves me.
cresc.
più cresc.
F
Cross the riv-er
f
mp
round the bend, How-dy stran-ger, so long friend, There's a

G7+ C9 G7 G7 Gm7 F
voice in the lone-some win' — that keeps whis-per-in' roam!
dim
sfz
(bravely)
C7 B♭ E♭m C7 Fdim F♯dim C7
I'm go-in' where a wel-come mat is, No mat-ter where that is 'Cause
f
F Gm Fdim C7
1. F
an-y place I hang my hat is home.
f
2. F
home.
f
p

COME RAIN OR COME SHINE
(From "ST. LOUIS WOMAN")

Words by JOHNNY MERCER
Music by HAROLD ARLEN

Fm6 Ebm6 Adim Abdim C7/G Edim Ebdim G7/D Db7 C9
But don't ev-er bet me, 'Cause I'm gon-na be true if you let me.
Fmaj7 F6 Ab7+5 A7 Dm A7+5 Dm7
You're gon-na love me Like no-bod-y's loved me, Come Rain Or Come Shine.
Bm7-5 B7 E9 A6 A7+5 Em7 Bb9 A9
Hap-py to-geth-er, Un-hap-py to-geth-er And won't it be fine.
D13 D7-9 D7 G7 D13 G7 Gm6 Dm7 Bm7-5
Days may be cloud-y Or sun-ny, We're in or we're out of the mon-ey, But I'm with you al-ways,
Bb9(#11) A7-9 D7 G13 C13 C13-9 Dm7 G13 Bb13 A7-9 Dm9
I'm with you rain or shine! shine!

The Girl That I Marry

Words and Music by
IRVING BERLIN

F7
B♭
C7
F7
girl I call my own will wear
B♭
Cm
B♭
F7
sat - ins and lac - es and smell of col - ogne. Her
B♭
Cm7
F7
nails will be pol - ished and in her hair, she'll wear a gar -
B♭
B♭9
den - ia, and I'll be there 'stead of flit - tin' I'll be

E♭
B♭dim
sit - tin' Next to her and she'll purr like a
B♭ Fdim F7 Dm F9 B♭ Fdim F7 Cm7
kit - ten A doll I can car - ry the girl that I
(kit - tin)
F7 Cm7 F7
1.
B♭ Cm7 F7 B♭
mar - ry must be. THE
2.
B♭ Cm7 F7 B♭
be.

Anything You Can Do

Words and Music by
IRVING BERLIN

CHORUS
G7 C G7 C G7 C
1. Annie AN-Y-THING YOU CAN DO, I can do bet - ter, I can do an - y-thing bet-
2. Annie An-y-thing you can buy, I can buy cheap-er, I can buy an - y-thing cheap-
3. Annie An-y-one you can lick, I can lick fast - er, I can lick an - y - one fast-
mp-mf
G7 C G7 C
ter than you Frank No you can't Annie Yes I can Frank No you can't
er than you Frank Fif - ty cents Annie For - ty cents Frank Thir - ty cents
er than you Frank With your fist Annie With my feet Frank With your feet
G C G7 Dm7 G7
Annie Yes I can Frank No you can't Annie Yes I can Yes I can
Annie Twen-ty cents Frank No you can't Annie Yes I can Yes I can
Annie With an axe Frank No you can't Annie Yes I can Yes I can
G7 C G7 C G7 C
An-y-thing you can be, I can be great - er soon-er or lat - er, I'm great-
An-y-thing you can dig, I can dig deep - er I can dig an - y-thing deep-
An-y school where you went, I could be mas - ter I could be mas - ter much fast-

G7 C G7 C
er than you Frank No you're not Annie Yes I am Frank No you're not
er than you Frank Thir - ty feet Annie For - ty feet Frank Fif - ty feet
er than you Frank Can you spell Annie No I can't Frank Can you add
G7 C G7 Dm7 G7 C
Annie Yes I am Frank No you're not Annie Yes I am, Yes I am
Annie Six - ty feet Frank No you can't Annie Yes I can, Yes I can
Annie No I can't Frank Can you teach Annie Yes I can, Yes I can
Em Em6 Dm Dm6
Frank I can shoot a par - tridge with a sin - gle car - tridge Annie I can get a spar - row with
Frank I can drink my li - quor fast - er than a flick - er Annie I can do it quick - er and
Frank I could be a rac - er quite a stee - ple chas - er Annie I can jump a hurd - le e -
D7 Am7 D7 Am7 D7
a bow and ar - row Frank I can do most an - y - thing Annie Can
get e - ven sick - er Frank I can live on bread and cheese Annie And
ven with my gird - le Frank I can o - pen an - y safe Annie With

G7 Dm7 G9 G7 C
(Spoken) (Sung)
you bake a pie? Frank No Annie Neith - er can I
on - ly on that? Frank Yes Annie So can a rat
out be - ing caught? Frank Yes Annie That's what I thought
An-y thing you can sing I
An-y note you can reach, I
An-y note you can hold I
G7 C G7 C G7 C
can sing loud - er I can sing an - y - thing loud - er than you Frank No you can't
can go high - er I can sing an - y - thing high - er than you Frank No you can't
can hold long - er I can hold an - y note long - er than you Frank No you can't
G7 C G7 C G7
Annie Yes I can Frank No you can't Annie Yes I can Frank No you can't
Annie Yes I can Frank No you can't Annie Yes I can Frank No you can't
Annie Yes I can Frank No you can't Annie Yes I can Frank No you can't
Dm7 G7 C
1.2.
3. Fmaj7 C
Annie Yes I can Yes I can.
Annie Yes I can Yes I can.
Annie Yes I can Yes I can.

HOW ARE THINGS IN GLOCCA MORRA

(From "FINIAN'S RAINBOW")

Words by E.Y. HARBURG
Music by BURTON LANE

Bb Fmaj7 Gm7 F Gm7 C7 Gm7 C7
Mor - ra? Is that lit - tle brook still leap - ing there? Does it still run down to
p mf
Gm7 C13 Gm7 C13 F Bb F Bb F Gm7/C
Don - ny cove? Through Kil - ly - begs, Kil - ker - ry and Kil - dare? How Are Things In Gloc - ca
Bb Fmaj7 Gm7 F Gm7 C7 Gm7 C7
Mor - ra? Is that wil - low tree still weep - ing there? Does that {lad - die / lass - ie} with the
Gm7 C13 C7 Gm7 C7
twink - lin' eye Come {whist - lin' / smil - in'} by and does {he / she} walk a - way, Sad and dream - y there not to

F C7 F A7 Bb C7 F A7
see me there?
So I ask each weep - in' wil - low and each
Bb C7 F A7 Bb Gm7 C7
brook a - long the way,
And each lad / lass that comes a - whist - lin' / a - sigh - in' Too - ra -
Fmaj7 D7-9 Gm Am Gm7 C7
lay
How Are Things In Gloc - ca Mor - ra this fine
1 F Gm7
day?
How Are Things In Gloc - ca
2 F
day?
mf

LOOK TO THE RAINBOW
(From "FINIAN'S RAINBOW")
Words by E.Y. HARBURG
Music by BURTON LANE
Moderately
mp
poco rit.
Very Slow
a tempo
Eb
Ab
Bb
Bb7
On the day I was born, said my fa - ther, said he, I've an
sump - tu - ous gift to be - queath to a child, Oh the
bund - led me heart and I roamed the, world free, To the
el - e - gant leg - a - cy wait - in' for ye, 'Tis a
lure of that song kept her feet run - nin' wild. For you
east with the lark, to the west with the sea; And I
rhyme for your lips and a song for your heart, To
nev - er grow old and you nev - er stand still, With
searched all the earth an I scanned all the skies, But
sing it when - ev - er the world falls a - part.
whip - poor - wills sing - in' be - yond the next hill.
found it at last in my own true love's eyes.

Cm Fm7 Bb7 Ebmaj7 Eb6 Fm7 Bb7
Look, look, Look To The Rain - bow, Fol - low it
mp
Eb Ab Cm6 Bb7 Eb Cm
o - ver the hill and stream. Look, look,
Fm7 Bb7 Eb Ab Bb7
Look To The Rain - bow, Fol - low the fel - low who fol - lows a
1,2 Eb 3 Eb Ab Eb Fm7 Bb7
dream. 'Twas a dream. Fol - low the fel - low, Fol - low the
So I
mf
Eb Ab Ebmaj7 Bb7 Eb
fel - low, Fol - low the fel - low who fol - lows a dream.
pp

OLD DEVIL MOON

(From "FINIAN'S RAINBOW")

Words by E.Y. HARBURG
Music by BURTON LANE

Abm Db7 Gb C7 F C7
To Coda
Old Dev - il Moon in your eyes.
Old Dev - il Moon in your eyes,
F Eb F Eb D F#m
You and your glance makes this ro - mance too hot to han - dle.
D Dm F+ Dm7 G7 C7 Bb
Stars in the night blaz - ing their light Can't hold a can - dle
Ebm
D.S. al Coda
to your raz - zle daz - zle.
CODA
F Eb F Eb
Just when I think I'm free as a
F C7 Eb F Eb F Eb F
dove Old Dev-il Moon deep in your eyes blinds me with love.
L.H.

If This Isn't Love

Words by E.Y. HARBURG
Music by BURTON LANE

C6
C+
C
dai - sy
plum - ber
With
I'm
mf
p
C7
moons all a - round
swing - in' on stars
And cows jump - ing
I'm rid - in' on
F
Fm
o - ver
rain - bows
There's
I'm
C
Cdim
Dm7
G7
some - thing a - miss, and I'll eat my hat If This Is - n't
bust - in' with bliss, and I'll kiss your hand If This Is - n't

C
F
To Patter
Love!
I'm
Fine
Patter
Dm
G7
Dm7
feel - ing like the ap - ple on top of Will - iam Tell; With this I can - not
B7
Em
D7
grap - ple be - cause, be - cause you're so a - dor - a - belle If
mf
mp
f
8va

A Fellow Needs A Girl

(From "ALLEGRO")

Words by OSCAR HAMMERSTEIN II
Music by RICHARD RODGERS

118
Cm Ab Eb/G Ab G Gb F
wrong, To hold in his arms, and know that she be-lieves that her fel - low is wise and
Fb Eb Ab+ Ab Bbdim Eb7 Ab+ Ab Bbm7 Eb7
strong, When things go right and his job's well done, He wants to share the prize he's won. If
Abm 8va Eb7 Dbm6 Eb7 Fm G7 C7 F B7
no one shares, and no one cares, Where's the fun of a job well done Or a prize you've
Bb7 Eb F/Eb Fm/Eb
won? A fel-low needs a home, his own kind of home, But to make this dream come
Cm Ab Eb F7 Eb Bb7 Bb7+5 Eb
true, A Fel-low Needs A Girl His own kind of girl, My kind of girl is you.
Ped.

THE GENTLEMAN IS A DOPE

Lyrics by **OSCAR HAMMERSTEIN** II / Music by **RICHARD RODGERS** **ALLEGRO** (1947)

hands down
up! The gen-tle-man gets me down!
R.H.
mf
L.H.
REFRAIN
A7
Dm
strongly
x arms
Dm6
The gen-tle-man is a dope — a man of man-y faults, — A
p-mf leggiero
B♭maj7
B7
C7
demonstrate
Dm
A7
clum-sy Joe who would-n't know a Rhum-ba from a Waltz. The
Dm
uncertainly
G7
demonstrate
gen-tle-man is a dope — and not my cup of tea. — (Why

distressfully
both hands
B♭maj7 B♭7 Dm E7 A7
do I get in a dith - er? He does - n't be - long to
mf
Dm Em7 A7 Dm
cooly
hand on head
me!) The gen - tle - man is - n't bright, he
mf
p
Dm6 B♭maj7 B7
knowingly
demonstrate
does - n't know the score A cake will come, he'll take a crumb and
C7 Dm A7 Dm
dreamily
gesture w/ one hand
nev - er ask for more! The gen - tle - man's eyes are blue but

G7
Bbmaj7
distressfully
lit - tle do they see
(Why am I beat - ing my brains out? He
mf
Dm
E7
A7
Dm
D7
does - n't be - long to me!)
He's
jealously
cross arms
G
Gmaj7
G6
G
C
3
some - bod - y el - se's prob - lem,
She's
spitefully
G
Gmaj7
G6
G
C9
wel - come to the guy!
She'll

convincingly
F Fmaj7 F6 F Bb Bbmaj7 Bb6 Bb
nev - er un - der - stand him half as
hotly
E7 E+ E7 E+ E7 A7(b9) A7 A7(b9) A7
well as I. The
mf
scathingly
Dm Dm6
gen - tle - man is a dope he is - n't ver - y smart He's
p
lovingly hug w/arms
Bbmaj7 B7 C7 Dm A7
just a lug you'd like to hug and hold a - gainst your heart, The

pleadingly
Dm
G7
gen - tle - man does - n't know How hap - py he could be
painfully
both hands
Bbmaj7
Bb7
Dm
E7
A7
Look at me! Cry - ing my eyes out, As if he be - longed to
mf
Fmaj7
Bbmaj7
Em7
A7
dejectedly
one hand up
Bm
G
D7(b5)
A7
me. He'll nev - er be - long to
1.
Dm
Em7
A7
me! The
2.
Dm6
Em7
A9
Dm
me!
f
mf
f
sf
8

PAPA, WON'T YOU DANCE WITH ME?

(From "High Button Shoes")

Words by SAMMY CAHN
Music by JULE STYNE

F
C
C#dim7
Pa - pa, take a chance with me And
G7
C
Dm7
C
D7/F#
Am7/G
D7/A
dance with me to - night. And when you
f
G
D7
G
whirl me 'round and 'round we'll go, Right off the
D7
G
D7
Am7/E
D7/F#
ground we'll go, A - round and 'round we'll go. And when we

G D7 G
hear the trom - bones slid - in' high We'll both be
D7 G G+ C7
glid - in' high up to the sky. I love the pol - ka.
F C C#dim7
Pa - pa, won't you dance with me? Oh,
mf
G7 C G7/B Gm/B♭ A7
dance with me, Please dance with me.

Dm
F♯dim7
C/G
D7
F♯dim7
When you hold me hold me tight. Oh, pa - pa,
C/G
Dm/G
C/G
Dm/G
C/G
C
Dm
C
Dm
C
G7
won't you dance with me to -
C
C7
C9
C7♭9
night?
C
A♭/G♭
Dm7/F
G7/D
C
F
C
night?

I Still Get Jealous

F9
F+
B♭
Cm7
I may not show it, but I
B♭
F7
B♭
Fm
G7
C7
F7sus
F7
do. It's more than I can bear
mf
B♭
D7
Gm
C7
when they start to stare. Guess they think you're too good to be
F7
Fsus
F7
B♭dim
B♭
F♯7
F9
true. I Still Get Jeal - ous when we kiss good -
p

Bdim F9 F+ B♭ Cm7
night Unless you hold me extra
B♭ F7 B♭ Fm G7 C7 F9 F+
tight. And, dear, I know a secret you
B♭ Dm A♭9 G+ G7 C7 C+ F7
didn't know I knew. I Still Get Jealous 'cause it pleases
B♭ B♭dim F7 B♭ F#7 B♭ B♭dim Cm7 F9 B♭
you. I Still Get you.
mf
p
rit.
f

ONCE IN LOVE WITH AMY

(From "WHERE'S CHARLEY?")

By FRANK LOESSER

Am7
D7
G
G#dim
Am7
D7
A - my,
Tear up your list, it's A - my.
G
C
G
Am7
G
Ply her with bon - bons, po - et - ry and flow - ers, Moon a mil - lion hours a -
B7
E7
Am7
D9
Gmaj7
C7
way. You might be quite the fick - le heart - ed ro - ver, So
Gmaj7
C9
Gmaj7
E9
Am7
D9
care - free and bold Who loves a girl and la - ter thinks it

Gmaj7
D
A7
D7
G
G#dim
o - ver And just quits cold, But once in love with
Am7
D7
G
G#dim
Am7
D7
G
A - my, Al - ways in love with A - my. Ev - er and ev - er
C
G
Am7
G
B7
E7
sweet - ly you'll ro - mance 'er. Trou - ble is, the an - swer will be that
Am7
A9
D7
G
A - my'd rath - er stay in love with me.

The New Ashmolean Marching Society And Students Conservatory Band

D D7 G
in - stru - ments in hand. There are those who
far - ther back you stand. But to me it's
G7/F C/E Cm/E♭ D7 G
fa - vor the phil - har - mon - ic fla - vor but to me the
bul - ly it sat - is - fies me ful - ly when I hear that
A7 D G G7/F C/E Cm6/E♭
fin - est in the land
thun - der close at hand
is
from
The New Ash - mo - le - an
mf
G G7/F C/E Cm6/E♭ G Am7 D
March - ing So - ci - e - ty And Stu - dents Con - serv - a - to - ry
1 G
Band. The
2 G
Band.
sfz

My Darling, My Darling

C7 F7 Bb G+ G7 Cm F7
My Darling, My Darling, I've wanted to call you "my darling" For many and many a
Bb Bdim C7 F7 Bb G+ G7
day. My Darling, My Darling, I fluttered and fled like a starling; My
Cm F7 Bb D Bm Bm7
courage just melted away. Now all at once you've kissed me And there's
Em D G A7 D G7 C7 F7
not a thing I'm sane enough to say Except, My Darling, My Darling, Get
Bb Dm7 G7 Cm7 F7 1 Bb 2 Bb
used to that name of "My Darling". It's here to stay. My stay.
mp
f

ANOTHER OP'NIN', ANOTHER SHOW
(From "KISS ME, KATE")

Words and Music by COLE PORTER

C13
F
an - oth - er show. An - oth - er job that you hope, at last,
Will make your fu - ture for - get your past,
F#dim
C7/G
C7
F
D7-9
An - oth - er pain where the ul - cers grow,
An - oth - er op' - nin' of an - oth - er show!
Gm7-5
C13
F
E7
Am
Am6
Four weeks, you re - hearse and re - hearse,
E
F#m7
Gdim
E7/G#
E7
Am
Am6
D#m
Am/E
F7
E
Three weeks, and it could - n't be worse,

E7 Am Am6 D7 C/E F#m7-5 G C C/B
One week, will it ev - er be right? Then out of the hat
C/Bb C/A D7 G7+5 C C7 F
it's that big first night! The o - ver - ture is a - bout to start, You
cross your fin - gers and hold your heart, It's cur - tain time and a -
F#dim C7/G C7 F D7-9 Gm7-5 C13 F
way we go, An - oth - er op' - nin' of an - oth - er show.
sfz

WUNDERBAR
(From "KISS ME, KATE")

Words and Music by COLE PORTER

G
are. Why, it's tru - ly wun - der - bar!
Wun - der - bar, wun - der - bar! We're a -
C
G
D7
lone and hand in glove, Not a cloud
G
near or far, Why, it's more than wun - der -
mf

Fm7
Bb7
Eb6
bar! Oh I care, dear, for you mad - ly,
mf
Fm7
Bb7
Eb6
And I long, dear, For your kiss. I would
Am7
D7
G6
G
C#m7-5
die, dear, for you glad - ly, You're di - vine, dear!
cresc.
f rit.
F#7
D9
G
And you're mine, dear! Wun - der - bar, wun - der -
p rall.
mp a tempo

C
G
bar! There's our fav' - rite star a - bove,
D7
What a bright shin - ing star, Like our
1
G
D7
love, it's wun - der - bar! Wun - der -
2
G
love, it's wun - der - bar!
rit.
f
p

So In Love

Words and Music by COLE PORTER

C C7-9 Fm C7 Fm
Even without you, My arms fold
poco marcato
p
Fm Bbm Eb Db Dbm
about you, You know, darling, why,
mf
Dbm Abmaj7 Ab6 Eb7 Db Eb7 Ab Db
So in love with you am I, In love with the
mf più espressivo
Eb7 Ab Db Eb7 Ab
night mys-te-ri-ous, The night when you first were there,
Ab Db Eb7 Ab Abmaj7 Ab6 C7 Fm Fm7
In love with my joy de-lir-i-ous When I knew that
cresc. più espressivo

Fm6
G7
C
C7-9
Fm
C7
you could care,
So taunt me and hurt me,
poco marcato
p
Fm
Bbm
Eb
Deceive me, Deceive me, Desert me. I'm yours
cresc.
f passionately
Eb7
Ebm6
F7
Bbm7
Bbdim
Ab
'til I die, So in love, So in love,
Abm
Abdim
So in love with you, my love am I.
dim.
f
poco allargando
p

Here I'll Stay

(From the Musical Production "LOVE LIFE")

Lyrics by ALAN JAY LERNER
Music by KURT WEILL

Cm6 G Cm7
Refrain (with warm expression)
F7 Fdim F7 Fm6
There's a far land, I'm told, Where I'll find a field of
p - mf
G7 Gm6 E♭m B♭ B♭m6
gold, But here I'll stay with you.
F7 E♭ Cdim Gm7 Cm7
And they say there's an isle deep with
mf
Cm7 F7 A7
clo - ver Where your heart wears a
R.H.

F7
Fm
G7
Cm6
Fdim
Cm7
smile all day through. But I know well they're
p
Fdim
wrong and I know where I be - long, And
Cm6
E♭m
A6
here I'll stay with you. For that
cresc.
f
B♭7
Gm7
G♭+
land is a sand - y il - lu - sion;
espressivo

B♭
Gm6
E♭m
It's the theme of a dream gone a -
Fm
G7
F
G7
Cm7
F7
Fdim
F7
stray,
And the world oth - ers woo I can
mp
B♭
Gm7
E♭m
F9
find lov - ing you, And so here
I'll
cresc.
f
1.
B♭6
B♭dim.
Cm6
Fdim
2.
B♭
B♭dim
B♭6
stay!
There's a
stay!
f

Bali Ha'i

Words by OSCAR HAMMERSTEIN II
Music by RICHARD RODGERS
Moderato
F Eb F G F G F
Most peo - ple live on a lone - ly is - land
Lost in the
mp f
8va bossa
8va
A G A G A F
mid-dle of a fog - gy sea.
Most peo - ple long for an - oth - er
Gb Ab Bb Ab Bb Gm7 C
is - land
One where they know they would like to be.
rit.
C7 Fdim F Fdim F
Ba - li Ha'i may call you an - y night, An - y day. In your
p mf

E Db7 F Db7 C7 F Fdim
heart you'll hear it call you: "Come a - way, Come a - way." Ba - li Ha'i will
F Fdim F E Db7 F
whis - per On the wind of the sea: "Here am I, Your spe-cial is - land! Come to
Db7 C7 F Bb Bb+
me, come to me!" Your own spe - cial hopes, Your own spe - cial
mf
3
Gm Bbm C7
dreams Bloom on the hill - side And shine in the streams. If you
mp
Fdim F Fdim F E
try, You'll find me Where the sky Meets the sea. "Here am I, Your spe-cial

Db7 F Db7 C7 F7 Bb C9 F6
is - land! Come to me, Come to me!" Ba - li Ha'i, Ba - li Ha'i! Ba - li Ha'i!
cresc.
mf
Edim Dm Edim Dm
Some day you'll see me, Float - ing in the sun - shine, My
mp
Gdim F6 Gdim Dm
head stick - ing out From a low - fly - ing cloud. You'll hear me call you,
Gdim Dm Gb Ab Bb Ab Bb Db Eb F
Sing - ing through the sun - shine, Sweet and clear as can be, "Come to
mf
C7 F6
me, Here am I, Come to me!" Ba - li Ha'i!
cresc.
cresc.
f

SOME ENCHANTED EVENING
(From "SOUTH PACIFIC")

Words by OSCAR HAMMERSTEIN II
Music by RICHARD RODGERS

Dm
E7
Am
C7
F
C
Dm7
You know e- ven then
That some- where you'll see her a-
As strange as it seems
The sound of her laugh- ter will
mf
G7
1. Cmaj7
C7
C+
Cdim
2. C
-gain and a- gain.
sing in your
dreams.
pp
G7sus
G7
Cmaj9
C
Dm7
G7
C6
C
G7sus
G7
C
Who can ex- plain it? Who can tell you why? Fools give you reas- ons,
tenderly and legato
Am7
D7
G
Adim
Edim
Dm7
Cdim
C
Wise men nev- er try.
Some en- chant- ed eve- ning
cresc. molto
mp
Dm7
G7
When you find your true love,

C
E+
Fmaj7
F6
When you feel her call you A- cross a crowd- ed room,
mf
C6
Dm
G7
Dm
E7
Am
C7
Then fly to her side And make her your own,
f
F
C
Dm
Dm7
G7
C
Or all through your life you may dream all a- lone.
molto espr.
rit.
dim.
a tempo
G7sus
G7
Cmaj9
C
Dm7
G7
C6
C
Once you have found her, Never let her go.
pp legatissimo
G7sus
G7
Cmaj9
C
Dm7
C
Once you have found her, Nev- er let her go!
rit.
mf
Ped.

YOUNGER THAN SPRINGTIME
(From "SOUTH PACIFIC")
Words by OSCAR HAMMERSTEIN II
Music by RICHARD RODGERS
Moderately
mp
molto rit.
C G F C G C G
I touch your hand and my arms grow strong. Like a pair of
a tempo
F C Bb Dm A7-9
birds that burst with song. My eyes look down at your love - ly
cresc.
Dm Fm6 C/G A7-9 Dm7
face And I hold the world in my em - brace.
f
mf

G7
C
G
C
G7
Dm7
G7
Young-er than spring-time are you, Soft-er than star-light are you,
molto rit.
p-mf
C
Am
Am7/D
D7
Gmaj7
G7
C
Warm-er than winds of June are the gen-tle lips you gave me. Gay-er than laugh-ter
p
G
C
G
Dm7
G7
C
Am
are you, Sweet-er than mu-sic are you, An-gel and lov-er, heav-en and earth are
Am7/D
D7
G
D7
Gmaj7
D7
you to me. And when your youth and joy in-vade my
cresc.
mf
cresc.

G
D7
Gmaj7
Dm7
Gsus
G7
arms And fill my heart as now they do. . .
then. . .
C
G
C
G
C
G7
Young-er than spring - time am I.
Gay - er than laugh - ter am I,
mp
cresc,
C
Am
Dsus
D7
G7sus
G7
An - gel and lov - er, heav - en and earth am I with
f
allarg.
1
C
G7
2
C
you!
you!
a tempo
f
dim.
morendo
p

THIS NEARLY WAS MINE
(From "SOUTH PACIFIC")

Words by OSCAR HAMMERSTEIN II
Music by RICHARD RODGERS

Eb
Fm
Eb
This Near - ly Was Mine
This Near - ly Was Mine
Ab
Ebm
Ab
Close to my heart she came
Eb
Bb
Eb
Ab
On - ly to fly a - way.
On - ly to
Eb7
Ab
F7
Bb
fly as day flies from moon - light.

Fm7
Bb7
Eb
Fm
Eb
Now, now I'm a - lone,
Bb
Bbdim
Ab
Still dream - ing of par - a - dise,
Abm
Eb
Cm6
Abmaj7
Still say - ing that par - a - dise
Cm6
Eb
Fm
Eb
Once near - ly was mine.

Let's Take An Old-Fashioned Walk

Chorus
Bright Valse tempo
C
Cmaj7
C6
Cmaj7
Dm
G7
F
Dm7
B7♭9
Em
mp-mf
LET'S TAKE AN OLD-FASH-IONED WALK I'm just burst-ing with talk
What a tale could be told if we went for an old-fash-ioned walk.
Let's take a stroll through the park
Down a lane where it's dark and a heart that's con-trolled may re-lax on an
old-fash-ioned walk.
I know for a

Gaug Em7 A9 G
coup-le who seem to be miles a-part,
There's
Em7 Am7 D7 G7
noth-ing like walk-ing and hav-ing a "heart to heart."
C Cmaj7 C6 Cmaj7 C Cmaj7
I know a girl who de-clined Could-n't make up her
Dm G7 C F C Dm
mind She was wrapped up and sold com-ing home from an old-fash-ioned
1 C F C Dm7 G7
walk.
2 C F Dm7 G7 C
walk.

DIAMONDS ARE A GIRL'S BEST FRIEND

By LEO ROBIN and JULE STYNE

Gm7 C7 F
pen - sive jew - els;
keep their flick - er;
a tempo
Chorus
C7 F Bb F C7
A kiss on the hand may be quite Con - ti - nen - tal But
There may come a time when a lass needs a law - yer, But
F Fdim Gm6 C9b C7 D7 Gm
Dia-monds Are A Girl's Best Friend,
Dia-monds Are A Girl's Best Friend,
A kiss may be
There may come a
D7 G Am7 Gdim G Am7 G7
grand But it won't pay the rent - al on your hum - ble flat Or
time When a hard boiled em - ploy - er thinks you're aw ful nice, But

C9 Gm7 C9 C7 F9 Fdim F9 B♭ A
help you at the Au - to - mat. Men grow cold as girls grow
get that "ice" or else no dice. He's your guy when stocks are
mp
B♭ B♭dim F A7 Dm G7 C7 F C7
old And we all lose our charms in the end. But
high, But be - ware when they start to de - scend. It's
F Cm6 Am7 D7 Gm7
square-cut or pear-shape, These rocks don't lose their shape, Dia-monds Are A
then that those lous - es Go back to their spous - es, Dia-monds Are A
cresc.
C9♭ F Fdim C7 F C7 F B♭6 F
Girl's Best Friend. A
Girl's Best Friend.
f mf f

BYE BYE BABY

By LEO ROBIN
and JULE STYNE

B♭6 G Cm G7 Cm7 F7♯5
ba - by! Lon - ta - na sem - pre te ne
ba - by! Re - mem - ber you're my ba - by
B♭ B♭dim7 B♭ Gm7 C7
vai, o ba - by per - chè?
When they give you the eye,
F7 B♭ D7 Gm B♭m7
Ep - pur lo sai che nel cuor por - ti un po'
Al - though I know that you care, Won't you write
mf
E♭ G7 Cm F7 D♭dim7 F7/C
del mio cuor e mai tu po - trai
and de - clare That though on the loose,

F7
B♭
A♭dim7
E♭/G
F7
li - be - rar - ti da me!
You are still on the square,
B♭
F7♯5
B♭
G7
Cm
G7
Bye bye, ba - by! Pe - rò do -
I'll be gloom - y, But send that
mp
Cm7
F7♯5
B♭
B♭dim7
B♭
Gm7
vun - que te ne an - drai, o ba - by, io
rain - bow to me Then my shad - ows will
Am7
D7
Gm
F♯dim7
Fm7
so che sem - pre a me pen - se - rai
fly, Though you'll be gone for a - while
mf

B♭7 E♭ Cm/E♭ A7♭9/E
per - ciò ti di - co "ar - ri - ve -
I know that I'll be smil - ing
B♭/F Gdim7 Cm7/F F7♭9 1 B♭ Em7♭5 A7♭5/E♭
der - ci, ba - by, tor - ne - rai!
With my ba - by bye and bye."
dim.
Dm7♭5 G7♭5 Cm7 F7 2 Dm7/A Dm7♭5 G7 G7♭9
rai! Tor - na
bye," With my
f
Cm Cm7 F7♭9 B♭ E♭ B♭
pre - sto, bye and bye!
ba - by bye and bye.
p

EARLY

F

A

Co

If we're not watching a Reagan sitcom, we're watching a Reagan Western. The black-hat boys from the Evil Empire pull into town on the afternoon stage, and Dutch stands at the end of the dusty street, spurs jingling as he fingers his Peacekeeper missile. But the dramatic showdown scene inevitably ends up on the cutting-room floor as Dutch smiles at his adversaries and tries to out-communicate them instead.

Reagan's best movie role was in *Kings Row*, in which his character, after discovering he was the victim of an unnecessary amputation, uttered the line, "Where's the rest of me?" In his current role in "Presidents Row," we ask, "What year is this?"

RONALD REAGAN

IN

"THERE YOU GO AGAIN
AND AGAIN AND AGAIN
AND AGAIN AND AGAIN AND
AGAIN AND AGA AGAIN AND
AGAIN AND AGAIN AND AND AGAIN AND
AGAIN AND AGAIN AND AGAIN AND AGAIN AND AGAIN"

Z

1 The 1984 Reelection

THE SAPPY WARRIOR

Fritz Mondale was rather like the Japanese soldiers from World War II who are periodically discovered on some remote South Pacific island, living off centipedes and coconuts, refusing to believe that the war is over. Mondale was the last New Dealer hiding in the jungle from his captors. He found out the war was over the hard way.

But didn't we see Walter Mondale's act in 1968, when another Minnesota senator and vice-president was the Democratic presidential nominee? Walter F. Mondale, the Humphreyesque Happy Warrior who, like the Minnesota Vikings, couldn't win the big one.

Fritz Mondale's entire Minnesota political career was patterned after and nurtured by Hubert H. Humphrey. Like Humphrey, Mondale was eventually defeated by having been the second fiddle in a southern Democrat's wildly unpopular administration. Mondale, ironically and prophetically, ran Humphrey's primary campaign. Mondale even attempted to borrow Humphrey's speaking style, although that was probably why Hubert lost in 1968.

Mondale, the Methodist minister from Lake Wobegon, resplendent in the gray steel-wool suit he was wearing at birth, tried to tell the American people, duped by Big Everything—except government—and oblivious to the sin and self-indulgence all around them, to repent.

But he was facing a TV evangelist who preached against sin while winking at it, and the viewers/voters had the volume turned down.

WIMP...
HHH
MONDALE
FERRARO

A WOMAN'S PLACE IS IN THE WHITE HOUSE

Gerry Ferraro was a '50s mom. She hung out in the kitchen trying to keep the cookies from burning while dumb old dad (played by Walter Mondale) was out wearing out his shoe leather trying to make a sale. Then Wally and the Beaver (played by 75 million voters) came stomping in, shoes muddy, and asked if there was anything in the fridge.

"I want you boys to wash your hands, clean your room, cut the grass, weed the garden, wash the car, write your grandmother, do your homework, and be nice to special-interest groups," the June Cleaver of the Democratic party announced.

"Aw, Mom, do we have to? All the other guys are out havin' fun teasin' minorities and blowin' their lunch money on BB guns, and all that other neat junk," Wally and the Beav responded.

"I don't care what all the other guys are doing. When your father gets home, you're really going to get it."

"From that wimp?"

...All the other guys are spending a trillion on defense, cuttin' taxes, and that other fun junk...right, Beav?
Gee... I don't know, Wally...
DAILY Democrat
DOOM
ARMAGEDDON
CHAOS
GLOOM
WAR
HATE
DISASTER
U.S.A.

DOES HART IMITATE LIFE, OR LIFE IMITATE HART?

Gary Hart has a hobby: sculpting birds from clay. His hobby has extended into his career, where he is now sculpting himself from an amorphous mass into a heroic bust of John F. Kennedy.

In the 1950s, Gary Hartpence, a shy, gawky college student from Kansas, decided that he didn't like his last name. His schoolmates called him "Hot-pants." So he decided he would discard "-pence" for the more syllabically conservative, politically pleasing "Hart." An uncle speculated that he was shortening his name for political reasons even then; voters like short, punchy, hard-consonant names, but there is probably no truth to the rumor that Hart will amputate his name to Gary Ha in 1988.

Hart has picked up the melody of the 1960s but not the lyrics. He is The Candidate of the Future, as Jack Kennedy was in 1960, but he is going to have a tough time inspiring the electorate to get misty-eyed about microchips and the trade deficit. But Hart has the JFK mannerisms down: hands nervously thrust into the jacket pocket, emerging only to jab a forefinger into the air, a wispy but convincing Kennedy coiffure, and an orthodontically orthodox row of white incisors.

Hart is also a rather adept amateur impressionist. He does Jack Kennedy very well. Hart has not worked out an impression of himself yet.

CAMELOT HINTS

PUSH COMES TO SHOVE

In Jesse Jackson's mind, he is somebody: the Reverend Martin Luther King, Jr. Jackson has enthralled transfixed audiences with his tale of how King, on that wretched day in 1968, died in his arms. This is all very moving, of course, except for a minor detail: it didn't happen. This may well have been one of the reasons that even Coretta Scott King endorsed Mr. White Bread himself, Fritz Mondale.

Jackson actually is a better orator than King was, but King's sincerity and serenity came shining through his rhetoric. Jackson comes across like an alliterative late-night TV car salesman. He is attracted to television lights like a kind of electronic moth.

One of Jackson's most outspoken supporters in 1984 was the Reverend Louis Farrakhan, a man who thinks Adolf Hitler was an okay guy who had a clumsy PR operation. Farrakhan called Judaism a "gutter religion." He then called upon his supporters to "smite" *Washington Post* reporter Milton Coleman because he reported that Jackson called New York City "Hymietown." Democrats fight, but they rarely smite. Jackson finally smote Farrakhan—weakly, without really exposing his pal's true agenda—figuring it was better to smite than snitch.

To his credit, Jackson is articulating many themes that regular—okay, white—politicians don't usually address, such as the permanent underclass and other nontelegenic topics. In spite of all this, Jesse somehow always ends up standing between the issue and the camera, casting a shadow that blocks the rainbow.

SELMA • I HAVE A DREAM •
MLK
I WANT TO BE KING...
...AND PRESIDENT.

AROUND THE WORLD IN '80s DAZE

John Glenn went from being The Right Stuff to The Wrong Stuff faster than it took him to orbit the earth. During the 1984 presidential campaign, he appeared to lose all radio contact with Mission Control, and to have had his personality replaced with an on-board computer.

Glenn tried to retro-rocket us back to 1962, when he graced the majority of *Life's* magazine covers, water-skiied with Jackie Kennedy, and orbited the earth three times with his knees in his nostrils.

But there was another problem: no one remembered that he had been a greater hero in real life than Ronald Reagan had been in *Hellcats of the Navy.* The crucial rock video viewer vote, according to some polls, thought he was the pilot of Jefferson Starship. Glenn had the corollary problem of being drab. Of course, he looked shinier in his silver space suit. He was not infrequently introduced at rallies as the first man on the moon, and upon completing a speech that would have sounded better punctuated by bursts of static, some local informed citizen would ask him if astronauts really drank Tang. By the time Glenn noticed the warning lights, he was wondering what color his parachute was.

There was some speculation from those who think Hollywood is the center of the solar system that Glenn's candidacy would benefit from the release of the film *The Right Stuff.* Unfortunately, fewer people voted for Glenn than saw the movie, which was about as many people as you can stuff into a space capsule.

Poor John Glenn. He was beaten by Walter Mondale, whose most exciting ride in 1962 was driving his Rambler to Duluth.

OUSTON, WE'VE
OT A PROBLEM...
MONDALE!
Glenn
7
WE WANT
MONDALE
OUR
HERO
FRITZ
'84
FRITZ
OUR
HERO
Frit
FRITZ
FRITZ
FRITZ '84
HERO
Z '84
FRITZ

ICON of the '80s

It is not difficult to define what era the Reverend Jerry Falwell wants America to return to. There are those who would argue that he's shooting for somewhere in the mid-Victorian era. The really uncharitable feel the 1600s in Salem, Massachusetts, is the Right Reverend's time frame of choice.

It is not a mental strain to envision the Reverend Mr. Falwell at the business end of a dunking stool, trying to drown the witches out of a wanton America:

> "Witche! Thou hast been engaging in the chewinge of Gumme, the imbibinge of spirituous Liquide, the readinge of licentious Smutte such as *Huckleberry Fynne,* votinge for liberal politicians who weare the Scarlet Letter of D for Democratte, mockinge Reagan and Helms, and not purchasynge the Kruggerrand! How do you pleade, Hellhounde?"
>
> "Glub."
>
> "Heathen! Now for the sentencynge! Thou shalt observe with Frequencie the Old Time Baptist Gospel Hour on cable television for eternity!"
>
> "Okay! I give up! I'll reform! Anything but that!"

SON OF A...
...WITCH!

2 | That's Not Entertainment

ROCKY HORROR PICTURE SHOW

Sylvester Stallone makes movies that bring us back to the way it wasn't. The first Rocky movie—there is no credible evidence to suggest that there will be a last Rocky movie, either—was a seemingly innocent affair, even with the underlying racial tension and the desire to construct a celluloid Great White Dope. In fact, the Rocky flicks were basically harmless if mindless, like movies of the '30s and '40s: small-mind boy makes good, gets girl, The End.

Then Stallone tired of just making films in which molars flew and noses flattened. He then made *Rocky IV,* which created the myth of Soviet technological superiority, when in fact everyone knows—except Stallone—that they can't build a digital watch any smaller than a manhole cover.

Stallone also made *Rambo,* in which one actor—sweaty pectorals flexing as he seemingly wipes out most of metropolitan Hanoi with a machine gun—cheapens an entire decade of American military effort and the deaths of 58,000 soldiers. Which is more disgusting—the fact that Stallone made millions off of this tripe or the fact that he apparently didn't take the Vietnam War as seriously as he does now by somehow managing to stay out of the service—is a matter of profound conjecture.

Stallone brings us back, but for all the wrong reasons.

STRANGER IN THE RIGHT

In 1961, Frank Sinatra, liberal Democrat, performed at the inauguration gala for a president of Irish descent.

In 1981, Frank Sinatra, conservative Republican, performed at the inauguration gala for a president of Irish descent.

Whoops, there goes another rubber creed. Does this man have any ideology whatsoever, other than to be a Friend of the President? The man keeps coming back and coming back and coming back. He endlessly cultivated Spiro Agnew when it appeared he was a leading contender for the presidency—that alone should have disqualified him as a political arbiter.

But now we see Old Blue Eyes singing wildly off-key with Nancy Reagan, toupee ever so slightly askew, and showing up at the White House to receive the Presidential Medal of Freedom. They must have changed the criteria. If he can make it there, he can make it anywhere. Will President Reagan go to a casino opening in Atlantic City to repay the debt?

Start spreading the news. We want to have no part of it.

...START SPREADIN' DA NEWWS... I WANT TO BE A PART OF IT, NEW FRONTIER, NEW FRONTIER...
...START SPREADIN' DA NEWWS... I WANT TO BE A PART OF IT, NEW FEDERALISM, NEW FEDERALISM...

GO AHEAD, MAKE ME MAYOR

California, whose main export is fantasy, has once again provided America with another conservative Republican actor/politician who has co-starred with a simian.

Clint Eastwood, whose greatest cinematic tour de magnum force is a string of movies featuring the NRA poster boy, Dirty Harry, was elected mayor of Carmel-by-the-Sea, California. Eastwood spent $45,000 to win an office that pays about $200 a month. For a fistful of dollars more, he could have a shot at a bigger role which would enable him to wield weapons that have buttons instead of triggers.

Eastwood denies any further political aspirations, but should we believe him? After all, Eastwood is the same age Reagan was when he first won office in California. Both men starred in Westerns: Eastwood in the spaghetti variety and Reagan in the forgetty variety. Both men shoot things off before thinking: Eastwood from the hip and Reagan from the lip.

Although the American people may not be ready—yet—for the sudden impact of an Eastwood administration, it would be nice to have a better actor in the White House.

GO AHEAD, GORBACHEV... MAKE MY DAY...
LOVE, MAGGIE XXX
PRESIDENT EASTWOOD
The BUCK gets BLOWN AWAY Here!

PLAY IT AGAIN, SAM

ICON of the '80s

"Let's go to the videotape"—an expression that was formerly the province of sportscasters—could now just as well replace In God We Trust as the national motto. Now that videocassette recorders are less expensive than a decent color TV set, America can rewind its past instead of moving fast-forward.

It is bad enough that we spend six or seven hours a day watching network dreck, but now we can waste all of our days transfixed to the tube harboring the illusion that the tapes we watch are worthwhile, merely because we have made the show selection instead of some druids in network programming. If we want to have Jane Fonda work out for us, we have that option instead of the nasty alternative of having to break a sweat ourselves.

Instead of flipping a channel, we have to drive to the video store—and woe to the person with Beta, since possessing a Beta machine is a little like being a Republican in Cook County—and pay to watch the stuff that used to be free on the networks.

A peculiar phenomenon is the fact that most people rent movies that they have already seen. If you are a film buff to start with, you will still go to the theater anyway, and then a year later pay to see the movie again in its VCR incarnation. This creates the feeling that we're living life on a kind of continuous tape loop, a Möbius strip that plays our lives over and over again.

Call it déjà viewing.

...Honey, what time is it ?
...1942.
BOGEY
VCR
1942

3 | The Past Is Prolonged

THE FIRST PRE-EXPERIENCED YEAR

In 1948, George Orwell wrote the futuristic novel *Nineteen Eighty-Four.* In it, Orwell presents a totalitarian state governed by "Big Brother," a video omnipresence impossible to escape. For thirty-six years hence, any event remotely reminiscent of the Orwellian prophecy was described as "being like 1984."

The fact was, of course, that no one knew what 1984 was going to be like, but it felt as if we had already lived through twelve miserable months of the most dreaded year in history. When it finally came, it was the world's greatest anticlimax, Halley's comet excluded—another pre-event that didn't quite live up to its buildup. Those who wanted to find the parallels found them, and there were some, to be sure. For instance, there are now television screens in practically every room in every residence in the United States, but they are more likely to be showing a dog food commercial than the glowering visage of Big Brother.

1984 went by rather uneventfully. Ronald Reagan, more of a Big Uncle than Big Brother, disposed of Walter Mondale, Weak Sister. And that was about it, except for Mary Lou Retton's 500-watt klieg-light incisors. Still, 1984 was the first year that had been completely pre-experienced, we could have gone right from 1983 to 1985 and not missed a beat.

And that was the year that wasn't.

estroy the
nstitution
order to
ave it.
Ed Meese

GOOD
OVERNMENT
HROUGH
DETECTORS
1984? LIKE ORWELL? C'MON, DON'T BE RIDICULOUS...
Information Through Secrecy
Peace Through Missiles
BALANCED BUDGETS THROUGH DEFICITS
NO NEWS IS GOOD NEWS

THE SURREAL THING

One of the simplest pleasures in life used to be the purchase of a nice, frosty Coca-Cola from a machine. You would put in your dime, open the glass door, and yank out a 6-ounce green bottle filled with America's nectar. Now things are more complicated.

First, they exchanged the green bottles and sometimes recalcitrant machines for cans and dispensers that require night classes in electrical engineering. These can machines have control panels that rival 747 cockpits for sheer complexity, and the odds are slightly less than hitting all six numbers in the New Jersey Lottery that your correct change will be returned. Recently, the Coke folks developed a dispenser that actually talks to you, a kind of combined HAL 9000 computer-carbonated Big Brother. Put in your 50 cents: "That's very good, Dave." Thank you, HAL.

Then the ultimate idiocy was perpetrated: one of Coke's marketing Bright Lights decided that the American people were tired of the tangy, slightly acidic flavor of their beverage. So the Old Coke was eliminated in favor of the New Coke, an ersatz syrupy impersonation of Pepsi. Then things got really complicated.

In the beginning, there was Old Coke, and it was good. Then Old Coke begat the New Coke, and the New Coke begat Coca-Cola Classic, formerly the Old Coke. Then there was Diet Coke, Caffeine-Free Diet Coke, Caffeine-Free New Coke, Cherry Coke, and Diet Cherry Coke.

Choke.

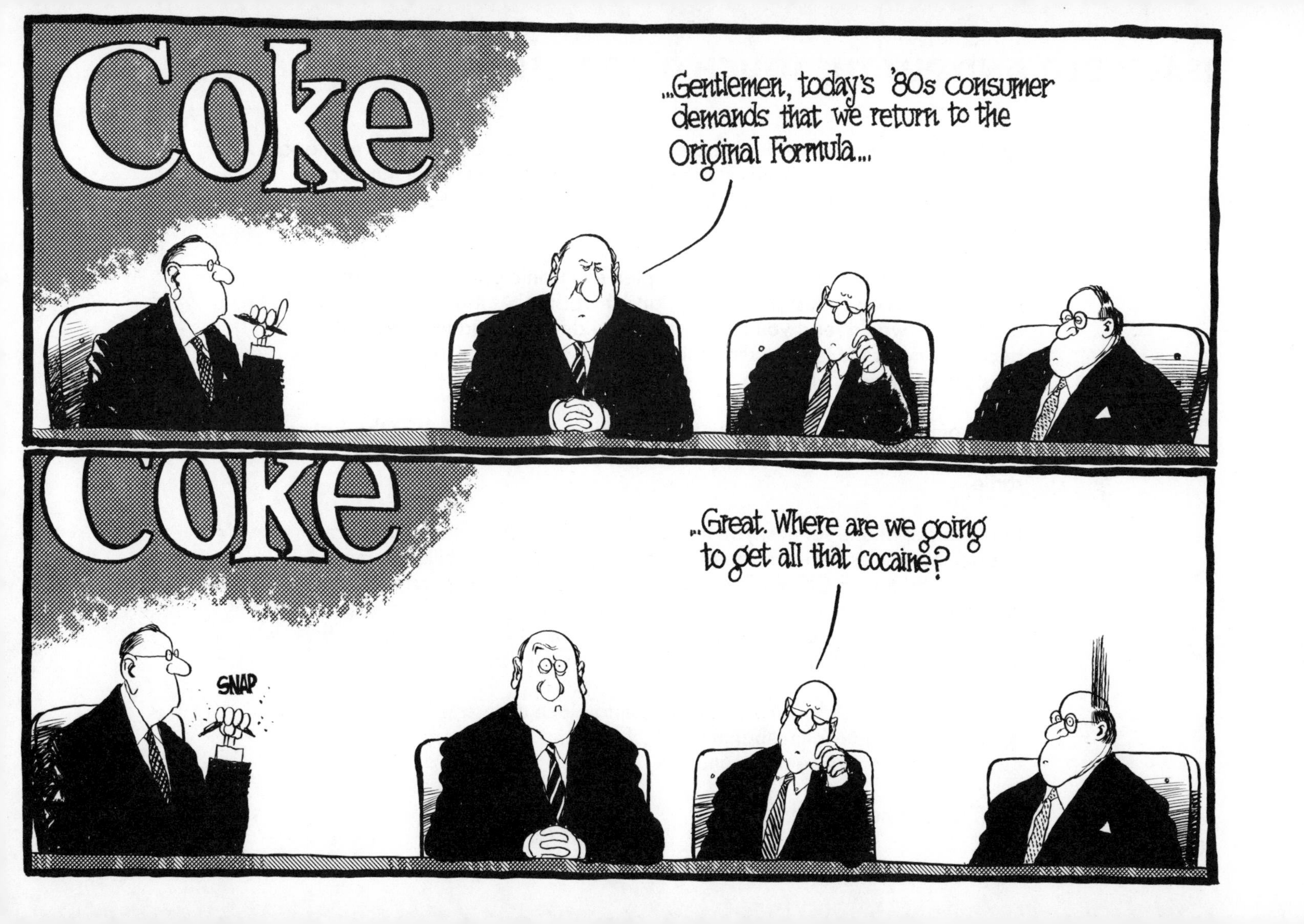
Coke
...Gentlemen, today's '80s consumer demands that we return to the Original Formula...
Coke
...Great. Where are we going to get all that cocaine?
SNAP

REACH OUT AND PUT THE TOUCH ON SOMEONE

On the surface, the Justice Department's breakup of the AT&T monopoly seemed to be a victory. People love to see Goliath take the occasional rock in the forehead. But this time, we may have dialed the wrong number.

The phone, for such an incredibly complex electronic ganglion, was as easy to use as a fork: you just picked it up, and it worked. At the end of the month, Big Mother would send you a bill, which you dutifully paid lest you wished to become one of the few genuine social pariahs in America: The Person Who Was Cut Off from Civilization.

Then some of the yellow-tie boys who had time on their hands at the Justice Department decided to start a class project. Our lives would never be the same.

Now, to get phone service, you have to . . . choose! Now there are three phone companies for every one Princess-style phone. The bills are more complicated than a Chinese income tax form. You have to purchase phones now instead of renting them; get a cheap one, and it's like talking into a garbage can. The operators' voices now sound oddly mechanical, like they have been replaced by the pods in *Revenge of the Body Snatchers.*

The result is chaos. Now it is more difficult to place a person-to-person call to Aunt Pooh in East Moline than it is for E.T. to get a clear connection. We now have the phone service of around 1898.

AT&T, phone home!

Phone
...You want to phone home? What's your local phone company, you know, the way it used to be?
E.T.&T...

FIREPOWER AND FLOWERPOWER

Fifteen years ago, G. Gordon Liddy would have probably pistol-whipped LSD prophet Timothy Leary on sight. Recently, this oddest of couples tour the college campus lecture circuit like a retro road show, reaping big bucks for educating America's youth about terminating people with extreme prejudice and eating purple microdot acid.

There's something for everyone in this firepower/flowerpower dog and phony show. For the nascent brownshirts in the audience, Liddy regales proto-totalitarians about the joys of covert operations and large-caliber weapons. For the students who major in chemicals, Leary is there to add perspective on the days of Tangerine Dreams and Marmalade Skies.

Liddy speaks giddily of the days when he offered to "sanction"—okay, let's dial "M" for murder here—columnist Jack Anderson. Leary, his mind left in a brown paper bag somewhere long ago, occasionally checks in to see what condition his condition is in.

G. Gordon Liddy's most famous exploit was holding his shooting hand in a candle flame. While aghast Washington dinner guests observed the impromptu flambé, someone asked Liddy, "What's the trick?" Liddy replied, "The trick is not minding."

Watching these guys is like holding your hand in a candle flame, too, except it's impossible not to mind.

TERMINATE, WITH EXTREME PREJUDICE!
HALLUCINATE, WITH EXTREME PREJUDICE!
I ♥ SF
CLEAN FOR GENE
MOBE

AND THEY CALLED IT YUPPIE LOVE

THE DRILL. The traditional date as it was presented in popular culture in the 1950s consisted of—if you were a male—putting on a suit and tie, pulling up to the front door of your date's house, and shaking her father's hand (firmly, so he wouldn't think you were . . . you know). Then, it was a quick drive to the Biograph to see *A Summer Place,* and then over to Pop's for a vanilla malted (two straws, natch), and then home—by eleven—for a kiss on the cheek and a shyly muttered: "Gee, you're swell."

THE PILL. The advent of the Pill in the '60s changed all that, of course. Dating as we knew it ceased to exist. The New Morality—or lack thereof—obliterated the rules. Sensational literature of the time—like *Life* magazine—devoted cover stories to communal living, open marriages, wife swapping, bed hopping, group sex, and other pursuits of the times calculated to shock the silent majority. Those who persisted in the old style of courtship lived in mortal fear of being found out, so they usually married quickly and took assumed names like "Ed" and "Betty."

THE CHILL. Various new strains of painful and/or fatal venereal diseases ended the sexual revolution at the close of the 1970s. Promiscuity was out, chastity—or at least selective chastity—was in, thus forcing a new way to approach the opposite sex. Then, a sexual therapist who was rapidly losing clientele discovered a way to help his patients work out the tensions that marked the end of the sexual revolution. He prescribed dating—old-fashioned, corsage-and-candy dating—as the antidote. The trouble with all this is that people have forgotten how to date.

THE BILL. But there are lots of people out there who will be glad to teach them—for a fee. For $19.95 (hardcover) they will counsel you on topics ranging from how to find a date, what to do on a date, and how to ditch your date. (Or, if you're tired of dating, *How to Find a Spouse in 30 Days.*) You can use up your MasterCard limit achieving the right Date Look. And one of those romantic evenings out on the town can set you back more than you used to spend on a year's worth of Trojans.

Love may be free, but dating isn't.

1950s...
WHY DON'T WE CALL IT A NIGHT?
1960s...
...WHY DON'T WE DO IT IN THE ROAD?
1970s...
...WHY DON'T WE DO IT TO BARRY MANILOW?
1980s...
...WHY DON'T WE GET A BLOOD TEST?

WHERE HAVE ALL THE FLOWERS GONE?

In the 1950s, the criteria used to judge a man's character were based largely on how neat his yard looked. If a man kept his lawn trimmed to putting-green length and texture, terminated with prejudice any alien weed growth, and dumped tons of mammal excretion on his flowerbeds, then that man was a true American. If a man relied on passing herds of sheep and other hoofed ruminants to keep his lawn down, then he would be turned over to the House Committee for Un-American Activities for further investigation.

In the 1960s, priorities changed. Having a neat lawn wasn't so important; relating to and grooving with nature in its natural state was in. Lawns stopped being mowed, they just . . . happened. Crabgrass was no longer Suburban Enemy Number One. It was just part of the macro-yard ecosystem.

In the 1970s, yards resembling Southeast Asia were passé; they were replaced by rock "gardens" and wood chips. Weird meandering paths, bubbling fountains, and huge pumice boulders were rampant. Yards suddenly had the look of a set from a hostile planet on "Star Trek."

But now we are comfortably back to the old standards established by sensible denizens of 1950s suburbia. Crew-cut hedges, geometrically perfect edges, and leaf-free lawns are now the designer yards of the 1980s. People who in the 1960s would have been more likely to discuss the violent overthrow of the United States government than mulching are now hanging out at the garden stores, rapping about Lawn Boys and urea.

It's the same old fertilizer all over again.

THE UNKINDEST CUT OF ALL

ICON of the '80s

Senator Phil Gramm of Texas and Senator Warren Rudman of New Hampshire were the architects—or, more properly, demolition experts—intent on returning the United States government to its roots. That is, back to the days when it didn't exist.

They are from states that do not cotton to Big Government: the New Hampshire state slogan is Live Free or Die, usually perceived as an anti-Inside-the-Beltway sentiment, and Texas is a mini-nation that favors federal intervention only on oil-depletion questions.

The whole problem with the Gramm-Rudman amendment—Grim Reaper to the bureaucrat who envisioned his department's expiration date on a granite slab—was that if all the budget cuts it called for actually happened, the next president of the United States would have been an IBM desktop computer. Granted, a computer may be quicker on its feet than the current Oval Office occupant, but we'd miss Reagan's quips and bloopers.

The amendment would have balanced the budget just as surely as driving a Chevy into a brick wall will stop that knocking and pinging noise under the hood—crude, but effective. After 1991, the Nostradamian year when all wailing and gnashing of teeth emanating from Washington was to have ceased, there would have been peace and quiet and balanced ledgers in the capital.

And the concept of the United States would finally have been as it was in 1776: a nice idea, but nonexistent.

Heck, we just want to get Washington back to its roots...
RAMM
RUDMAN

To Be Erected
On Thiſ Site
City of Waſhington D.C.

4 All The President's Men

BULL IN THE WHITE HOUSE CHINA

Don Regan, the former Merrill Lynch chairman, is bullish on America. And why shouldn't he be? He runs it.

Regan plays Wall Street to Ronald Reagan's Main Street: both streets run through beautiful downtown 1938. Regan is the banker; he handles the mundane mechanical transactions while Reagan—the small-town optimist speculator who didn't learn from the crash—invests in harebrained schemes. Reagan says, "Sell," and Regan sells.

Regan dresses as if he stepped out of a 1930s Hollywood movie about a banker who is about to foreclose on six farm belt states. Regan has already foreclosed on several promising Washington careers, including former Health and Human Services secretary Margaret Heckler, who didn't listen when Donald Regan talked.

But other women listened when Regan, at the Vienna summit conference, said that women didn't understand complex subjects like nuclear weapons. Regan, the kind of man who reads *Playboy* along with his arms proposals, ended up nuking himself; the gender gap became a radioactive crater.

Don and Ron have a 1980s version of the 1930s Edgar Bergen–Charlie McCarthy act. Regan sits on Reagan's lap, but Regan's lips move when Reagan speaks.

Don Regan, after all, is no dummy.

STUMP SPEAKING

Theodore Roosevelt, who was perhaps our nation's most environmentally conscious president, saw at the turn of the century that America could be stripped bare of its trees and minerals by a swarm of entrepreneurial locusts. James Watt, who served the least environmentally conscious president, decided that Theodore Roosevelt was an environmental extremist.

Watt decided that he couldn't see the forest for all the trees, so he started a Washington, D.C., Chainsaw Massacre of federal lands. It's not nice to fool with Mother Nature, but Watt tried. Sure, a sunset on the ocean is nice, but it is even more stunning through a skyline of oil derricks. A mountain is pretty to look at, but a mountain with 3000 feet sawed off the top is something special.

Watt, after leaving office in a cloud of chainsaw exhaust and bark dust, wrote a book called *The Courage of a Conservative.* There is more irony in that title than James Watt probably intended. The definition of a conservative is one who conserves.

As a protector of the environment, James Watt is a wastrel liberal.

I'M IN SUBJUGATION HERE

Alexander Haig is, vis-à-vis the presidency and in terms of chief executivity, the first individual to verbalize his candidateality through an agent at the William Morris agency, conduitwise.

The administrationness of Richard Milhous Nixon will be the paradigm, scenariowise. The point in time will be 1974, in terms of chronological period reference. Exigencies in the geopolitical arena will be nonparametric: interlopers will be contained within the framework of termination with the highest possible prejudice. Congressionally speaking, guerrillas who undermine domestical tranquil status will interface with a commander-in-chief who is in control here.

Leadershipwise, Commander-in-Chief Haig will be the vicar of exo-American relationships. Obviating conflict personnel insertions may or may not be viable, if a nonpeace situation is desirable. Strategic, tactical, or theater fission implements may be in a state of implementation if ineluctable.

The news media, both electronic and nonelectronic, will interface with a stone wall.

HOW'S THIS?
KID, YOU'RE GETTING THERE.

THE FOUNDERING FATHER

Ed Meese, that noted constitutional scholar, is the nostalgic type. He pines for the days when James Madison and Company were hashing out the Constitution.

"Hi guys! I'm Attorney-General Meese. Need a hand with that clumsy document?"

"Attorney-general? Have we put that in the Constitution yet?"

"Yeah, Article One. Anyway, I'm here to give you some guidance on how to make the Constitution make sense two hundred years from now. Have you gotten to the Balanced Budget Amendment yet?"

"Balanced budget? How difficult can it be to balance? We've only got seven thousand dollars. Besides, that's your future problem, not ours. We're worried about Life, Liberty, and The Pursuit of Happiness."

"Hey, get with the eighties, Madison. Rights and liberties are out. We're into strict construction now. I'm here to make sure that you guys don't write ambiguous material about freedom and equality that may be misinterpreted by future attorneys-general such as myself."

"Good point. Franklin, take out the part in Article One about needing an attorney-general. It's obvious the ninnies two hundred years from now will just misinterpret the job."

...Did you guys put in the amendment about mandatory drug tests, tax breaks for segregated schools, school prayer, balanced budget, and lie detector tests yet?
We, the People

ARE YOU NOW OR HAVE YOU EVER BEEN A COLUMNIST?

Before Pat Buchanan was hired by the White House to explain to President Reagan what Reaganism was all about, he was without question the most histrionic of the conservative columnists in the country. If Buchanan didn't use the phrase "Marxist stooge" at least weekly in his column or on his television program, his fans could safely assume Communists were behind the omission.

Now Pat Buchanan toils in the service of the president, crafting his phosphorescent prose for a more soothing voice to deliver. But unfortunately the lines are distressingly familiar.

In 1950, Joe McCarthy, the junior senator from Wisconsin and not nearly as clever as Pat Buchanan, alleged in a speech in Wheeling, West Virginia, that there were 206 Communists in the Truman State Department. Later, there were 87 Communists or 175 Communists or whatever number Senator McCarthy deemed appropriate to the audience. These claims were later shown to be made out of whole cloth, but people believed McCarthy anyway. It was a simple concept: throw the bucket of slime and run; if your opponents disagreed, they were Communists, too.

Now, thirty years after McCarthy's passing, Pat Buchanan is back in the breach, letting Democrats know that either they are with the president, or they are card-carrying, dues-paid-up members of the Communist monolith.

Buchanan should know, however, that, while he's busy finding out if there are now or have ever been, President Reagan has a dangerously subversive past.

Reagan, after all, was a Democrat before he was a Reaganite.

...ARE YOU NOW OR HAVE YOU EVER BEEN A COMMUNIST?
GOSH... I WAS A REGISTERED DEMOCRAT ONCE... DOES THAT COUNT?

BARD OF EDUCATION

The secretary of education, one William Bennett (Williams, '65), is a classics buff. His theory of education is that if everyone reads and even, God forbid, understands the classics, then all will be right with the world. He is, however, in the service of a president who not only hasn't read the classics but has a library that appears to be arranged by color rather than by topic.

You remember the classics from high school. Shakespeare probably sticks out in your mind. William Bennett yearns for those days when Bill was Big, even though in order for kids to read the classics they must first learn some fundamentals, such as reading.

"Hark! Your Education Secretary-Bard doth speaketh. Ye who eschew mine edicts shall be damn'd to stupidity and car wash employ."

"Who are you, mister? I'm about to leave for my three-week California vacation in my 4 × 4 pickup with the 80-watt Blaupunkt, so speak your piece."

"Thous shalt be accurs'd, uneducated whelp. I command thee to stay home and read sonnets."

"Get with the program, Bennett. No one reads sonnets; they watch 'Miami Vice' and 'Moonlighting' and old movies on the late show. Now buzz off before I bean you with a copy of *TV Guide.*"

"Pardon mine impertinence. I dids't not recognize thou, uh, Mr. President."

amlet & Hamitup...
CUT STUDENT LOANS, BILL!
ALAS, POOR STUDENTS, WE KNEW THEM WELL...
BENNETT EDUCATION

APHRODISIAC OF THE '80s

ICON of the '80s

In the 1960s, it was not fashionable to be overly concerned with the pursuit of the Almighty Dollar: making stoneware was more desirable than making interest. But in the '80s, money has become Topic A.

In the '60s, money was discussed only in the context of contempt for those who had it, or was something you wrote Dad for so that you could spend another semester sitting in the university president's office. People talked about ending the war, stopping the draft, electing Gene, dumping the Hump, turning on, tuning in, dropping out, but they never, ever, talked about money.

Now people talk about money as if it's actually an interesting topic: "So I leveraged a loan at two points above prime, socked it away into some really sweet tax-free munis, and then plowed the interest into IRAs, Keoghs, and a Fannie Mae." Spiritual gurus have been replaced by economic gurus; we have gone from prophets to profits. Gag me with a T-bill.

Sharp advertisers with an eye for—you guessed it—a buck have now made money a selling device. Cigarettes are now for the most part encased in gold boxes, and so, too, shall be their heavy consumers; beer ads revolve around "having it all," presumably excluding a beer gut and a couple of DWI citations; charge cards are now offered in the gold variety which, in turn, requires you to pay the interest charges in gold ingots.

Money has very nearly replaced sex as an erotic topic. In one commercial, a woman langorously invites a man to try out her new VISA card as if it were some sort of economic sex toy. We are living in a material world, and she is a material girl.

Money used to be the root of all evil. Now it's the root of our lives.

Sex Toys of the '80s

5 The Happy Media

U.S. A-OK!

The folks who bring you *USA Today* are happy people! They want you to feel good about America, like we did at the turn of the century! So did William Randolph Hearst! They're optimistic! So was William Randolph Hearst! They love exclamation points! So did William Randolph Hearst!

USA Today wants you to be happy people, too! They want you to think that everything is A-OK in the USA! They want to make news fun! Like TV! That's why all their newspaper boxes look like 26-inch Sony Trinitrons! Reading *USA Today* is just like watching TV! There's never anything good on!

USA Today is a quick read! So is a cereal box, but a cereal box usually has more in-depth coverage! They have lots of neat headlines in *USA Today* like this: "We're Feeling Good/About Weenies and Beanies!" Real news stories go inside! Real news stories are complicated and do not lend themselves to cute headlines! Real news is no fun!

USA Today wants to rename the United States the "USA," because it rhymes with more words than "United States"! The phrase "United States" has probably never appeared in *USA Today,* so you see a lot of stories about "President of the USA Ronald Reagan"! It's a quicker read! It's more fun!

So if you don't have a lot of time to read—and who does with all that good stuff on TV?—read *USA Today*! It's your right!

You can look it up in the USA Constitution!

JUST LIKE TV — THE NATION'S OBSEQUIOUS RAG — 35 CENTS

PAGES OF TEMPS FROM PAGO PAGO

WEATHER! Hell yes, enough to gag the chief of the National Weather Service

Color weather radar with Doppler Unit inside

PUBLISHED BY VIDKIDS

NANCY: NOT AGING A BIT
GRATUITOUS INTERVIEW, 1A

TV: IT'S FUN
INANE ANALYSIS, 1B

OBLIGATORY DAILY PORTRAIT OF DUTCH

MONDAY, WE HATE MONDAY, DON'T YOU?

NEWSLIE

A QUICK READ FOR THOSE WHO CAN'T

NUCLEAR WEAPONS: USA Defense Secretary Cap Weinberger says that the USA needs more nuclear weapons, and that's jake with us.

PUPPIES AND KITTENS: USA fuzzy puppies and kittens are cuter than ever, and they're expected to stay that way.

DICK AND JANE: See Dick. See Jane. See Dick and Jane read US,A Toady. It's at about their reading level. See Spot. See Spot use it properly. Bad Spot!

We're sucking up to Reagan more than ever!

By Fawn Cozy
US,A TOADY

WASHINGTON – A poll of the US,A Toady staff shows we're snuggling up to the president.

- We run at least one front page color oil painting making the USA president look like he's 33 years old.
- We headline his every pronouncement as if it was a new commandment in the Bible.

Our glorious Gipper

THE USA PRESIDENT - Airbrushed Photo

In March of 1981, the Era of Walter drew to a close. And somebody—the poor sucker—had to replace him. It was more than a job—the candidate had to become The Most Trusted Man in America in time for the next ratings sweep. And CBS chose Dan Rather, the man who smarted off to President Nixon.

Dan Rather found himself in the wholly unenviable position of attempting to stay within the spirt of Cronkite, while also being forced to create his own niche. His first attempt to break away came during the first few months, when his ratings took the inevitable slide. This was at least partially due to his hyper-strident delivery; Rather could make a three-point drop in the Dow send investment bankers scurrying for the ledges. He then figured that wearing a warm fuzzy sweater would make him seem warmer and fuzzier, too. But it was more like putting booties on a robot.

Dan Rather had to answer the question of who he was. Edward R. Murrow? Not cerebral enough—that's Koppel. He finally settled on . . . Lyndon B. Johnson.

Johnson! That's the ticket! The turning point for Dan Rather, Texan, came on election night, 1982. He shed the appearance of a man speaking to you from the inside of a fish tank, looking all bug-eyed and talking loudly to get your attention. He went to . . . Mr. Texas! LBJ! Bigger'n all outdoors! He reeled off election results like he was in a cowboy bar in El Paso! "It's tighter than a tick in the Texas governor's race!" "The Republicans look like they've been rode hard and put away wet!"

And that's the way it is. Pardner.

...HAS ANYONE UNPLUGGED DAN YET?
BS
VENING
EWS

JESUS LOVES ME, THIS I KNOW, FOR THE BABBLE TELLS ME SO

Pat Robertson, the Phil Donahue of televangelists, possesses a television network—Christian Broadcasting Network, or CBN—that employs almost otherworldly state-of-the-art satellite and communications technology to bring America true spiritual enlightenment. Robertson hosts "The 700 Club," which is kind of like the Phil Donahue show without the polymorphous pan-sexuals. In addition to "The 700 Club," viewers can experience true spiritual enlightenment through reruns of "The Best of Groucho Marx" and "I Married Joan."

Whether or not one can get a minimum daily requirement of theology through watching "The 700 Club"—and who are the 700, anyway?—is a question best left to those who ponder the Larger Questions, like Nielsen. But why run moldy 1950s reruns? Can the meaning of life be found through Dobie Gillis? Will moral awakening take place on "Love That Bob"?

You hear a lot of anti-Communist talk on CBN, not to mention innumerable commercials about The Word. But if CBN is really going to be effective in fighting communism, they'd better stop showing programs featuring Marx. And the word? The word that gets the most play on CBN is a secret word, one you hear every day.

Say it and win a hundred dollars.

AND THEN THE PROFITS...ER, PROPHETS CAME UNTO ME...
7
CBN
1-800-SEND BUX

NO NEWS IS OLD NEWS

The news media, when they run out of real news, or become bored with the news they already have—famine, disease, pestilence, and other nonphotogenic topics—are increasingly turning to news that has already occurred to fill up dead air or empty space.

The device the news media use to re-report just the facts, ma'am, is the anniversary. The nice thing about anniversaries is that you can create a news story when none exists. In recent years, we have observed the 40th anniversary of Pearl Harbor and the dropping of the A-bomb on Hiroshima, the 20th anniversary of the assassination of John Kennedy, the 10th anniversary of the resignation of Richard Nixon and the end of the Vietnam War, and practically every other event that can fill the time slot on "Nightline," "20/20," or "60 Minutes."

In the '80s, there is no new news; we're just recycling news stories. Political corruption, a staple item of the 1970s, is now so commonplace that there have been enough members of Congress incarcerated in the last ten years to form a jailhouse of representatives. There are so many wars being fought that casualty figures are reported as laconically as college football scores—"Druse 56, Shi'ites 47 in overtime." Middle East mayhem is no more stunning than yesterday's weather forecast. America is becoming anesthetized to today's news; yesterday's bulletins are denuded of their shock value and are therefore infinitely less appalling.

Today is the anniversary of the first day of the rest of your life.

ABC NEWS NEW
HI MOM
GOOD EVENING. THERE IS NO WORLD NEWS TONIGHT, BUT SOME INTERESTING THINGS HAPPENED 40, 25, 15, 10, AND 5 YEARS AGO TODAY...

LIP MAN OF THE '80s

George F. Will, who is the only television commentator with the guts to wear a bow tie, is perhaps as ubiquitous a TV presence as Mr. Whipple, the man who can't stop squeezing the toilet paper roll while he loudly protests the similar actions of others. Will is not unlike Whipple: he will declaim an action of the Reagan administration immediately preceding an intimate dinner with his friend the president.

Will was also involved in the first pre-experienced presidential debate—at least for Ronald Reagan. Will assisted then-governor Reagan in preparing for the encounter with Jimmy Carter; David Stockman portrayed Carter in the dry runs and destroyed the hapless Reagan's arguments, thus providing an early warning sign for Reaganauts that went unheeded. On television after the 1980 Carter-Reagan debate, Will pronounced Reagan the winner, adding somewhat excessively that the former actor performed in the manner of "a real thoroughbred." What Will didn't reveal until later was that he was the jockey.

Will is a kind of electronic Walter Lippmann, as he would probably be more than happy to acknowledge. Lippmann, the dean of political columnists for thirty years, would often rather give advice to a president personally than just let Ike or Lyndon read it like other mere mortals. Will has a similar modus operandi: he shuttles easily between lunch with Nancy and eating Reagan for breakfast on "This Week with David Brinkley." Will should know this behavior is not unlike being a White Sox fan and a Cubs fan simultaneously. It's a good way to get a black eye in both Comiskey and Wrigley.

Take a stand, George. Make a decision. White Sox or Cubs?

...GOOD ANSWER, GEORGE...... "THERE YOU GO AGAIN, JIMMY."...
Carter Briefing Book

CLOSE ENCOUNTERS OF THE NERD KIND

ICON of the '80s

Remember the high school math nerds you teased mercilessly? You called them names: Weenie, Grind, Dork, Geek, Drip, Dink, Twerp, and other clever appellations you thought were uproariously amusing at the time. Now that they are in charge of all the bombs, they have a name for you: Soft Target.

You tweaked the horn-rims off their pimply noses and you turned them down for dates. They all stuck together, though. They plotted revenge while you were out throwing a football around or going to cheerleader practice. They met in tiny cliques and slid their slide rules and figured out pi to the 178th decimal place.

Then Ronald Reagan was elected; more likely than not you voted for him because he was a winner, like you were in high school. The nerds probably voted for the nerd who ran against him. But then Mr. Popularity, the new president, decided that we needed something called "Star Wars." You thought, "Oh, how cute. Like the movie."

But the nerds knew. They knew he was talking about laser beams and particle weapons and throw weights and hundreds of other ways to send you from condo to cave in fifteen minutes flat.

They remembered what you did to them way back then. Now they're in charge of all the bombs.

Who's the weenie now?

...I'VE SEEN "STAR WARS" 136 TIMES!
U.S. AIR FORCE
BE WITH YOU.

6 | Retrogate In '88

THE CHRYSLER IMPERIAL PRESIDENCY

It seems these days that everyone is gaga over the prospect of an outspoken, politically naive auto executive being put in charge of the U.S. nuclear weapon arsenal and everything else under the purview of the presidency. But haven't we been along this road before?

Remember George Romney?

George Romney was the Lee Iacocca of the 1960s, minus the cigar and the Anglo-Saxon rejoinders. He was everything Iacocca is—an auto executive who headed American Motors and gave us the Rambler—and, as a Mormon, thought he might go to hell if he drank coffee. Everyone loved the guy; President Kennedy was said to have thought that the only person who could have beaten him in 1964 was Romney. By the time Romney began his presidential campaign he was the man to beat. But then he opened his mouth; he said he was "brainwashed" by the Johnson administration on Vietnam. He was finished after that.

If Iacocca is elected, he will be obliged to write "Iacocca II," which may go something like this:

> "Things really went downhill after Gorbachev told me he didn't like me anymore. I had to borrow a trillion bucks from the IMF to pay off the deficit, and they're charging higher interest than VISA or MasterCard. I turned all the defense contracts over to Chrysler, which is now building tanks with ugly two-tone color schemes and door handles that magically turn into a handful of screws and metal when you open them.
>
> "Then I got the offer to leave the presidency of the United States to become president of Albania. Sure, it's a failing country, but I think I can turn it around."

The Chrysler recall...
ROMNEY
'68
IACOCCA 1988

THE NEO-DEAL

While Alabama politicians may doubt the electoral viability of someone named Mario, there are those who feel that America also may not be ready to elect someone named Billy Joe Bob or Goober.

Cuomo is now talked up as the latest savior of the Democratic party, although there is arguably nothing left to save. His highly regarded keynote address at the Democratic Convention in 1984 extolled the virtues of the family, but Geraldine Ferraro may wish to take issue with him on that score.

Now Cuomo comes to us as a New Deal governor of New York, ready to rescue the country from the doldrums of a narcoleptic chief executive. Cuomo's Rooseveltian Rose Garden strategy could work, but the country is not standing in a bread line and Wall Street businessmen have not as yet been spotted on their ledges taking some air. Another problem is that Reagan beat Cuomo to the punch: he ran against Jimmy Hoover. Reagan has since exchanged this persona for Eisenhower's, which is less demanding and permits the president to watch prime-time network TV with impunity.

Even money says that the Democrats will once again nominate a northern FDR clone. Cuomo will ring all the bells and pull all the switches, and then go on to carry the District of Columbia. The Democrats will once again re-create their electoral Black Tuesday and crash.

Happy days are here. Again.

The Democratic Party today nominated the Governor of New York for the Presidency.
Gov. Roosevelt pledged a commitment to the family and blasted Wall Street.
The NEWS
IT'S FDR

The Democratic Party today nominated the Governor of New York for the Presidency.
Gov. Cuomo pledged a commitment to the family and blasted Wall Street.
The NEWS
IT'S MARIO

LADIES AND GENTLEMEN, THE PREPSIDENT OF THE UNITED STATES

George Bush—you remember, Vice-President George Bush—has the distinction of serving, after President Reagan's surgery, as the first acting president of the United States, taking the reigns of power for a few heady moments while Don Regan was out getting a cup of coffee. Well, actually, Ronald Reagan was the first acting president, but Bush was the second. However, the Connecticut Yankee is taking acting lessons from the First Ham himself.

There is no more unlikely a Reagan impressionist than George Bush. Reagan has the dulcet tones of an easy-listening FM radio announcer. Bush sounds like a Chipmunks record played backward at 78. Reagan looks comfortable in blue jeans and cowboy shirts. Bush looks as if his Brooks Brothers rep tie is three good yanks too tight. The man just can't pull it off.

The reason Bush is attempting this Reagan rip-off is that the president has become an instant retro-relic, an Eisenhower of the 1980s who is nostalgia personified. Any politician in the late 1980s would be wise to emulate the president, at least on a stylistic level. But Bush winds up playing priggish Felix Unger to Reagan's Oscar Madison, the disheveled but likable dodo. The two men are the quintessential odd couple.

Bush is smart to try to hark back to an era that hasn't even closed yet. But Bush as Reagan?

Would Don Knotts play John Wayne?

Presidential Preparatory Academy Yearbook

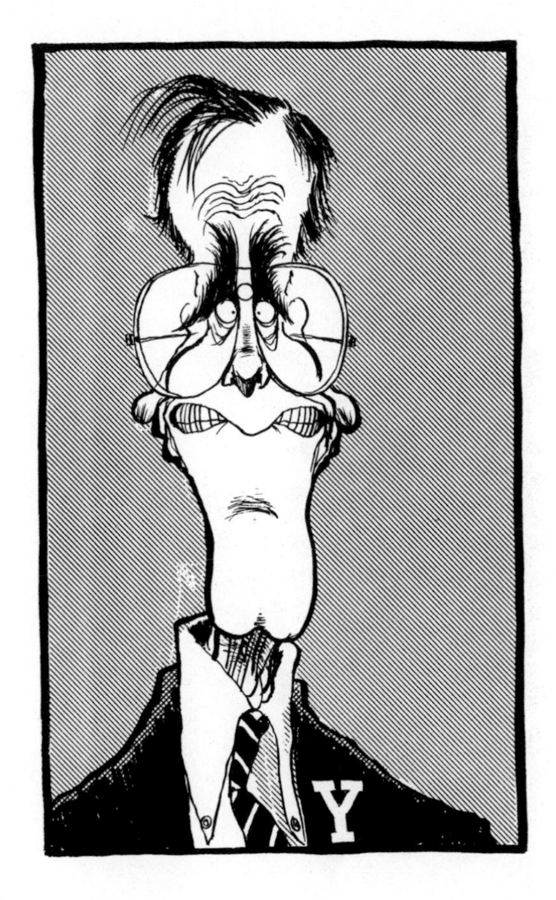

George Herbert Walker Bush

"Veep" "Cinderella"

Freshman Doormat, 1, Handmaidens, 2,3,4.
Political Eunuchs, 1,2,3,4. Whiners, 1,2,3,4.
Sycophants, 1,2,3,4. Ladies in waiting, 1,2,3.
Fall guys, 1,2,3,4. Bridesmaids, 1,2,3,4.
Second Banana, 2,3. Second Fiddle, 3,4.
Fifth Wheels, 1,2,3. Lap dogs, 1,2,3,4.
Brown Nosers, 1,2. Apple Polishers, 3,4.
Toadies, 1,2,3. Boot lickers 1,2,3,4.
Kowtowers 1,2,3,4. OPEC Fan Club, 4.

Quote: " They also serve who stand and wait."

THROWBACK QUARTERBACK

If Jack F. Kemp runs against Gary Hart for president in 1988, the American people may find themselves voting for the candidate who can hum the theme from *Camelot* most convincingly.

Give Kemp the edge on technical points. Jack Kemp's initials are, conveniently, JFK. His Kennedy mannerisms make Gary Hart look like he's doing Vaughn Meader. The man has even gone so far as to hire a woman who was a professional Jackie Kennedy look-alike as his personal secretary. Throw in the (touch) football angle, and the torch is passed. It's 1961 all over again.

Kemp is a kind of ideologue-savant economist; he scribbles notes in his playbook while right-wing economists bark plays from the sidelines. His latest retro-economics idea is the return to the gold standard, which was largely responsible for the Great Depression. This is a truly novel idea: all of our currency would be based on a metal found only in South Africa and the Soviet Union. One of Kemp's favorite economic saws is the JFK line, "A rising tide lifts all boats." A tide of red ink can also sink them.

Kemp is the quarterback who wants to move up to head coach. He has already begun to work on his inaugural address, with no help from Theodore Sorensen, JFK's former speech writer. It will go something like this: "The ball has been passed to a first-round draft pick of Americans."

OKAY, JACK... TRY IT ONE MORE TIME... "THE TORCH HAS BEEN PASSED"
AND THE RUNNING BACK IS DOWNFIELD IN THE END ZONE, SO HE ROLLS OUT LEFT...
TEXT
JFKemp

ICON of the '80s Shucks. It's been prit near forty years since ol' Yeager pushed the outside of the envelope and punched a hole in the sky with lil' ol' *Glamorous Glennis* and us folks are just now gettin' 'round to 'preciatin' it.

I mean, a fella hangs his hide out over the edge, straps a red-hot piece of machinery to his tail and hopes the sumbitch don't kinda like to blow up, and finally some . . . *kandy ass in a white suit, for chrissakes* . . . gets the idea to write a book about it. Then some . . . *goddamn Hollywood types* . . . make a movie, which admittedly kinda augers in, but, still! it makes the point, that's the thing!

The point bein' here that ol' Yeager, after flyin' and drivin' and drinkin' and flyin' some more, gets his just desserts after a buncha college boys get all the glory, just for bein' . . . *Spam in a can* . . . goin' up in a goddamn tin can with a parachute, and then they're hailed as the best pilots since Creation, all the while this ol' boy is doin' real flyin'.

Forty goddamn years later, and this here Yeager finally gets the credit. And a book royalty that'll knock your socks off, to boot.

Now that's the Write Stuff.

When you Broke The Sound Barrier, was it like...Being On Acid?
YEAGER
BELL X-1
GLAMOROUS GLENNIS

7 Talkin' About My Generation

HELLO MUDDA, HELLO FADDA, HERE I AM AT CAMP GRENADA

Young people, who are, unfortunately, still the final arbiters of what is in and what is not, have now decided that serving in the armed forces is once again fashionable. They have made this decision, obviously, because no one is in the process of being shot at on foreign soil.

During the '60s and '70s, the only reason for going into the armed service of your country was having a high draft number or being unable to convince the local draft board that your urine was always purple. Vietnam, of course, was the major raison d'outre, but a lot of it was simply a question of defying authority, particularly authority with guns.

Now authority—and the military—is Back In, Standing Tall. This can be partially explained by the lack of a nightly body count on the evening news, but credit should also be given to Hollywood for stepping in to fill the reality vacuum. Gone were the grim images of Lieutenant Calley and My Lai; replacing them were the upbeat images of Bill Murray in *Stripes,* Richard Gere in *An Officer and a Gentleman,* and Goldie Hawn in *Private Benjamin.* Military life was *fun.*

In truth, of course, Bill Murray would have been shot at dawn in Fort Leavenworth for singing "Doo wah diddy, diddy dum diddy doo" in the real army. Richard Gere would have spent a few decades peeling potatoes for decking his sergeant. Goldie Hawn would have been given a Section 8 and sent to the Fort Dix rubber room.

Besides the movies, even military clothing is in style; wearing camouflage and army boots with a shaved head is très chic. Army-Navy surplus stores are now the Bloomingdale's of fascism fashion. Though the gawkiest Camp LeJuene maggot didn't know it, he was In.

But how long will this popularity last—increased enlistment, the ability to spend $640 for a toilet seat with impunity—once shooting replaces shooting the bull?

Vietnam

Grenada
REAGAN '84
Rifle
Cleaning
Kit

BEWARE OF GREEKS BEERING SCHLITZ

The Greek system—a contradiction in terms—is more popular than ever. Once reviled in the '60s for turning out junior corporate pigs and alcoholics, the Greeks have staged a comeback thanks largely to the film *National Lampoon's Animal House.*

But the point that the kids who watched *Animal House* missed was that the movie did not glorify the Greek way of life—it dismembered it. The Deltas, led by John Belushi's bloated Bluto, were really neo-hippies. It wasn't a fraternity, it was a proto-commune. Had they picked up on this, campus observers would be writing about the return of the tie-dyed T-shirt and macrobiotic diets.

As John Belushi succinctly stated the case, "But nooooooo!" The college kids absorbed the wrong message. They styled themselves after the rival rich snob fraternity instead; college campuses are filled with surrealistically clean-cut preppy boys and girls who mirror the 1950s. Pipe smoking has replaced pot smoking, and the only haze—purple or otherwise—is to be found in inane initiation ceremonies.

While all is not lost—some frats are keeping within the spirit of *Animal House*: falling down drunk on 3.2 beer, throwing freshmen pledges for distance, and other higher callings—there are a lot of fraternities devoted to more urgent issues: who can we keep out?

Still, this insensitivity training will serve them well as they step out into the '80s, where exclusion is becoming all the rage once again.

ΤΦ
...HEY, BLUTO! WE'RE JUST LIKE YOU!!!
TWINKIES
TWINKIES

ASK NOT WHAT YOUR ORTHODONTIST CAN DO FOR YOU . . .

They are new, but not necessarily improved. In 1960, when JFK was running for president, doomsayers—who probably eventually turned their attention to the Zero Population Growth movement—predicted that if John Kennedy were elected, a 100-year Reich of Kennedys would be running for office and providing millions in revenue for orthodontists.

There are practically enough young Kennedys now running for office or at least thinking about it to elect a working majority of Kennedys to the House of Representatives. Those Kennedy kids are always getting into trouble.

They are everywhere now. *People* magazine is thinking about changing its name to *Kennedy* magazine, since 80 percent of the cover stories are now devoted to John Jr.'s favorite rugby ball or to Arnold Schwarzenegger, the only Republican Kennedy. No one has the guts to talk Conan the Barbarian into becoming a Democrat.

It was possible to watch toothy hostette Maria Shriver of the "CBS Morning News"—which has since lost the touch football morning ratings game—interview Arnold Schwarzenegger and Cousin Joe Kennedy in the morning, read about this week's Kennedy in the News in the afternoon—one is always passing or flunking the bar, going 97 mph in a 25 zone, or announcing or rejecting a candidacy—and then watch Ted Kennedy bellow stirring but incomplete sentences on the evening news.

Americans who thrilled to the clarion calls of the brothers in the '60s are finding the whole replay of the *Camelot* soundtrack a bit scratchy. The torch is past.

But it is nice to know, whenever we need a Kennedy fix, that there will be a couple hundred of them around to make us feel dentally inadequate.

DYNASTY II: THE KENNEDYS

GARBLED GARB

Fashions are one thing in life that are reliably cyclical: what comes around goes around. But with the advent of MTV and the instant fashion, a look that once took months to become nationally and sartorially acceptable is now available to us immediately thanks to the speed-of-light imagery of the rock video.

In high schools, where rock videos are studied with much greater enthusiasm than the fetal pig in Biology II, boys wear white T-shirts and jeans, madras shirts and shorts, black high-top basketball shoes; and even black leather—risky but correct in the '50s—is making a comeback. Girls are sporting caricatures of their mother's beehive bouffants, lace, and layers. Granny also has found herself relieved of her boots by would-be WannaBes. Everyone now wears the Ray-Ban Wayfarer, which were once the Official Nerd Sunglasses.

This look is known as "Mod"—this is getting to sound familiar—and now paisleys, Day-Glo earrings the size of stop signs, and other psychedelic accoutrements of the late 1960s are in. This look was made even more popular by Madonna ("Desperately Seeking Sixties"), while her Jimmy Dean-clone husband Sean Penn took up the slack in the white-T-shirt-and-sneer department.

The '80s look in the schools is really the look of the '60s, from the 1961 crew cuts to the 1968 psychedelics, all thanks to the immediacy of the fashion marching orders sent out from MTV Master Control.

Let's all pray that Madonna stays out of the maxi-dress, and that Motley Crüe avoids all contact with the leisure suit.

1960s

1980s

YIPPIE GOES YUPPIE

ICON of the '80s Jerry Rubin, who twenty years ago would have liked to take credit for the total destruction of Wall Street, had he been somehow able to accomplish it by merely having a big mouth, is now happily ensconced amongst the corporate fascists on the Street.

It is hard to believe that Jerry Rubin now works as a stockbroker; his defection to the real world—after being the putative leader of the unreal world for so long—was perhaps the most convincing sign for those of his generation that the '60s were really over, with the possible exception of Gene McCarthy's endorsement of Ronald Reagan in 1980.

Rubin, the Yippie who nominated a pig for president of the United States of America, who practically destroyed the Democratic party barehanded in the streets of Chicago, and who advised the youth of America that a valid political statement could be made by killing their parents, is now wearing the Wall Street Imperialist Lackey Running Dog Pinstripes.

It's . . . over.

KILL YOUR PARENTS!
OFF THE PIGS
YIPPIE

MAKE A KILLING.
YUPPIE

8 | Videodrone

THE VOICE OF A NEW GENERATION

You knew it would happen. You are under forty and in a bar with four or more Lite beers under your belt. Guess what? Someone starts singing television theme songs, and the next thing you know, you're involved in a rousing chorus of "The Addams Family" or "Car 54, Where Are You?"

Of course, someone got the bright idea to sell these teletunes in a collection, and you're kicking yourself for not having thought of it everytime you struggle to remember that obscure line from "The Flintstones" theme. People who were born after 1945 seem to have cassette decks in their minds that play nothing but audio artifacts from the mindless blare of the tube. People don't really talk anymore; they speak in sound bites.

The one thing that links all people under forty is the common language of the sitcom theme or the Saturday morning cartoon jingle. Purging this electronic flotsam is impossible; it's like an audiovisual water torture, a kind of TV tinnitus. But it provides a common ground, a language of lunacy for those who may have nothing else in common.

So we burp up these songs in our leisure, as punctuation marks in non-conversation. It is easier to do this than to actually say something meaningful. It is entirely possible, in fact, to respond to nearly any query with a bit of TV trash.

Even our conversation is pre-recorded.

...THEY'RE MYSTERIOUS AND KOOKY, THEY'RE ALTOGETHER OOKY... THE ADDAMS FAMILY!!!
...KHRUSHCHEV'S DUE AT IDLEWILD...CAR 54, WHERE ARE YOU?
...MEET THE FLINTSTONES, THEY'RE THE MODERN STONE AGE FAMILY... FROM THE TOWN OF BEDROCK...
CHANGE THE @*!?! CHANNEL...
Sudz Lite
BLAT
Burp HEAVY

RERUNNING IN PLACE

Perhaps it was inevitable that the medium that brought us the rerun would create the re-rerun. Prime-time television, which once surreptitiously reused old plots and formulas, has now come out of the closet by simply remaking the oldies in a new image.

"I Dream of Jeannie," a program that won few plaudits in 1965, was released from the bottle again twenty years later—minus the talents of Larry Hagman, who portrayed an astronaut with The Wrong Stuff. The players of "The Andy Griffith Show" were reunited; once again, Barney was able to fumble for the bullet in his shirt pocket, Gomer and Goober—aggregate IQ still firmly in the double digits—were back at the filling station, and even Opie was back, sporting a receding hairline. Interestingly, this program was the seventh-highest-rated show in television history.

"Leave It to Beaver" characters were reunited, all original hams on deck except for Ward, who faded to black. Beaver, pudgy, fortyish, was divorced with two kids, while Wally and his wife—Yup City—were having trouble having children; Eddie Haskell was convincing as a sleazy home contractor, although it seems more likely he would have become a loan shark or a personal injury lawyer.

Watching these shows is like going back to your twenty-year high school reunion: you get to see who put on seventy pounds and who went bald. You compare your waistline to theirs and maybe feel a little bit older than you did before.

But why couldn't we assume that these people somehow made it through the years better than we did?

GEE, WALLY... WHAT ABOUT IMPOTENCE, THE PILL, TOFUTTI, BUSING, SPROUTS, ANIMAL PSYCHOLOGISTS, ROUGHAGE, COCAINE, THE NEW COKE, HERPES, NUCLEAR PROLIFERATION, ECSTASY, MTV, SINGLE PARENT FAMILIES, LATCHKEY KIDS, PRIMAL SCREAM THERAPY, HOT TUBS, TRANSSEXUALS, AND PHIL DONAHUE?
STUFF A SOCK IN IT, YOU LITTLE GOOFBALL...
B
W

HOWARD HUGHES, CABLE NEWS, AND THE BRAVES' NEW WORLD

Ted Turner—the owner of the Atlanta Braves, the Atlanta Hawks, WTBS, and a backyard lion—is probably the only person in America who could be declared an innovator for showing reruns of "Gilligan's Island." Of course, Ted Turner does most of the declaring about Ted Turner.

Ted Turner is Howard Hughes before he flaked out. Swashbuckling adventurer, media mogul, avid aquisitioner, Turner fits the profile: his attempt to take over CBS with paper and bravado is likely to be recalled as his Spruce Goose. Sometimes it seems like only a matter of time before Turner moves to Las Vegas and grows out his fingernails like a set of steak knives.

Humanity has spent thousands of years developing every conceivable method of communicating with each other. Cable television is the latest of these methods; Turner's cable network has brought us not the future, but Wally and Beav, Skipper and Gilligan, and other elderly creations of the Big Network Triumvirate that Turner decries.

Ward, I'm worried about the Turner.

...WE'VE DONE IT!!!
WE'VE GOT THE MOST
ADVANCED COMMUNICATIONS
NETWORK IN THE WORLD!
IMAGINE THE POSSIBILITIES!
...SKIPPER, MR. HOWELL'S
BEEN KIDNAPPED BY
A GORILLA!
Turner Broadcasting

SMILE, YOU'RE ON CANDID CHIMERA

Owning a home video camera demonstrates what is known as the "Hi, Mom!" phenomenon. Whenever an average person appears on camera, they stop acting like sane individuals going about their business, drop whatever activity they are currently engaged in, and mug wildly, yelling, "Hi, Mom!" when their mother isn't within a 1700-mile radius.

The theory behind the purchase of one of these contraptions is that you can record your friends and family as they are in real life. This is false. The red light goes on, and real life comes screeching to a halt. A family becomes a troupe—Dad raises his eyebrows wildly, Mom giggles hysterically, the kids grin uncontrollably, and the dog barks as if the Manson family is about to break in. The red light goes off, and everyone stops acting. Hi, Mom.

Having a tape library of our lives permits us to rewind our past to happier times, when our hairlines were intact and the kids were asking for Kool-Aid instead of the keys to the Volvo. We can even resurrect departed loved ones, like a video Lazarus.

The box Brownie camera used to perform this function for us. It is now a much maligned little instrument, but it had a sturdy dignity and allowed us to remember our past with a little loving fuzziness, instead of the jarring reality of the home video.

The Brownie is one thing worth going back to.

...TWENTY YEARS FROM NOW, YOU'RE GOING TO BE GLAD I DID ALL THIS...
TWENTY YEARS FROM NOW, I'M GOING TO BE GLAD THAT STUPID VIDEO CAMERA IS OBSOLETE...

ICON of the '80s

Bernhard Goetz, a man whom you would dismiss as a wimp just shortly before he'd fire a couple of .357 Magnum rounds at you, has restored a long forgotten word to the American vocabulary: vigilante.

Vigilantes did most of their really memorable work in the Old West before Big Shot Eastern Lawyers had a chance to extend the U.S. Criminal Code west of the Mississippi River. Vigilantes rode around on horseback, blasting away with Peacemakers until their idea of justice was meted out. Sometimes they were on the right track, but, if they weren't, wrongly accused parties were not physically able to appeal their sentences. If a case was thrown out on a technicality, it was because their bullet missed or the noose rope snapped.

Bernhard Goetz, who looks like Clark Kent's less assertive brother, decided on a New York City subway that he would no longer be a victim. To demonstrate his abdication of victimhood, he decided to empty his revolver into the next person or persons who gave him any lip. The four kids who gave him lip—they claimed that they had "asked" him for five bucks—ended up getting a fusillade of bullets for an answer.

Goetz rode into town on a white horse, spouting off to the assembled media multitude. Public opinion was with him, at first, a la: "We're mad as hell and we're not going to take it anymore." Then when it became clear that Goetz may have shot first and asked questions later, the once-supportive public left him for dead, just as he left his four would-be loan applicants on the subway floor.

Goetz saw himself as Gary Cooper in *High Noon,* wielding his piece for Truth, Justice, and the American Way. But Gary Cooper never shot himself in the foot.

DEW NOT "SPARE CHANGE?" ME, OH MAH DARLIN'...
GOETZ GETS YA
KOCH
RAOUL 83
SHARKS RULE
WHITE PUNKS
CHI CHI
HOWM I DOIN
NEW YORK PEST
VIGILANTE FOR GUV
READER POL
YES
macy

9 | Curtain Calls

THE RUSSIANS ARE COMATOSE, THE RUSSIANS ARE COMATOSE

The Soviet Union went through four leaders in three years, which is an even worse record than George Steinbrenner established in the same time period with the Yankees. The pre-Gorbachev leadership didn't just remind us of the past, they were the past.

Every year at the May Day parade in Red Square, the ruling members of the Politburo were yanked from their IVs and dressed in heavy black coats and wool hats. They were propped up in their chairs and instructed to move their ancient paws in little semicircles, pupils fixed and dilated, to demonstrate to the world that they still emitted brain waves.

And then there were the funerals. Vice-President "You die, I fly" Bush barely had to go back home to get fresh shirts when yet another photograph would disappear from the Kremlin wall. The Soviets would then display their dead leader like a halibut on ice for 500 million people around the world to see. Another halibut, green around the gills and listing slightly to starboard, would take his place at the May Day parade.

But now it appears the Soviets have learned the lessons of television; they installed as their leader the Russian version of John F. Kennedy. Anyone in the Soviet Union who wears wool suits and who has a wife who doesn't look like a 300-pound sack of flour is considered charismatic. At fifty-five, Mikhail Gorbachev is considered relatively youthful by world leader standards. He is positively prenatal by Politburo standards.

Now the shoe—once banged on a table—is on the other foot. The United States has the ancient leader. But even if the Kremlin has the new kid on the block, they still have the geriatric politics of the bloc.

THIS IS THE WAY LENIN WOULD HAVE WANTED IT...
IS THAT TRUE, COMRADE?
ONE UNIT
CCCP

A CHECKERED PAST

You could get a million dollars. I know where it could be gotten. All you have to do is resign in disgrace from the presidency, lay low for a couple of years, come out of hibernation slowly, do TV interviews for hundreds of thousands of dollars, and sell the literary equivalent of historical docudramas to book publishers.

Richard Nixon has Saved the Plan.

We keep having Richard Nixon to kick around again, and again, and again. Oddly, he seems to enjoy it. Nixon enjoys not only living in his own past, but re-creating it in his own image right before our eyes.

And we watch him, like we slow down on the freeway to see an accident; we are ashamed and repulsed, but we look. And he charges admission, like the old days when he was barker at the Slippery Gulch Carnival. And we pay—attention, money, whatever he wants.

Nixon is rather like the Bhagwan Shree Rajneesh of foreign policy. He sits on the throne in his good Republican cloth robes and free-associates streams of geopolitical gobbledygook, while we, the disciples, listen raptly. We take whatever solemn nonsense he intones as gospel, and buy his books of sayings, and watch his video visage glowering at us.

And when we leave, full of thoughts about hey-you've-gotta-admit-he-was-a-great-foreign-policy-guru, he cashes his checks.

But it would be wrong, that's for sure.

YOU WON'T HAVE NIXON TO KICK AROUND ANYMORE...
...DON'T YOU WISH.

EX-CALIBER

Ted Kennedy, The Last Prince of Camelot, The Keeper of the Flame, The Bearer of the Torch, is a King Arthur in exile: his six attempts to pull Excalibur from the stone have been consistently thwarted by The Lady in the Lake.

For one brief shining moment, there once was a spot known as Camelot. The Last Prince was a mere courtier then, a man who would be King. Then it was abruptly, grotesquely, over; the King was cut down by a churl.

The Last Prince suddenly became The Lost Prince. His heart was in the battle, but not his head. He spent too much time at the banquet table and not enough time at the Round Table. His armor rusted, his sword tarnished, his legions shrank.

By the time he finally donned the armor and picked up the sword, the crusade was almost finished. All the king's horses and all the king's men couldn't put him back together again; then he lost his only real fight to Jimmy, The Court Jester.

The Last Prince was once the leader of the liberals in the kingdom. Now he is abdicating, unwittingly, to Jesse Jackson—The Man Who Would Be King.

We asked for it. We really did. We were tired of having chronic liars as president, so we elected Jimmy Carter, Who Never Told a Lie. Jerry Ford was really not intelligent enough to lie, but he pardoned the Great Prevaricator, and that was close enough.

Carter tried to bring us back to those halcyon days when presidents didn't lie, although you probably have to go back to George Washington to find one of those. So we believed him. Or we wanted to believe him. Until he told us that we were having a crisis of confidence and we had to give up our hot tubs and high times. Then we stopped believing him, and looked for someone who would tell us that it was okay to be mortgaged up to our nostrils and feel good—no, rejoice!—about consumption. Enter Reagan, stage right.

Jimmy Carter's homey homilies about Good Guvmint and presidents who were pathological dissemblers weren't as reminiscent of a rumored time in our past as his appearance was. He would stare into the television cameras with electric blue eyes and suddenly it would register with you just where you had seen this guy before. Carter looked like Eleanor Roosevelt in drag.

Jimmy Carter, an untelegenic prophet without honor, was overthrown for a movie actor who destroyed him with the words, "There you go again." Reagan unwittingly uttered the phrase that set the tone for the 1980s: here we go again.

Plain
Plains

AN ECHO OF 1967

January 28, 1986, dawned sunny but cold on Cape Canaveral. The space shuttle Challenger, plagued by innumerable delays, sat on the launch pad, not far from where Apollo 201—manned by Gus Grissom, Ed White, and Roger Chaffee—was consumed by a flash fire on January 27, 1967.

There was no indication of trouble. Disaster always seems to strike in the most banal settings. The space program had almost seventeen years of near-perfection since the fire on Apollo 201. The space shuttle had become as routine as the Eastern Shuttle.

This particular flight, however, was the focus of unusual attention, due to the presence of social studies teacher Christa McAuliffe, the first true civilian to be selected to fly in space. The crew was unusual in its own right: with an Oriental man, a black man, a Jewish woman, and three white men in addition to McAuliffe, it was almost a rainbow coalition.

Finally, at 11:38 A.M., the Challenger rose almost haltingly from the gantry. A ground controller, laconically reciting telemetry data, paused briefly when an "S"—meaning static, or no data—appeared on his screen with no explanation. He then looked at his monitor and saw grotesque curlicues of rocket exhaust and fragments of the shuttle plummeting to the Atlantic Ocean. Shock made his tone mechanical: "Obviously a major malfunction. We have no downlink." Later, films of the launch would show a sinister puff of black smoke from the right solid rocket booster joint. The flight of the Challenger lasted 73 seconds.

The shuttle tragedy shattered forever the last vestige of our naive faith in the infallibility of our space technology. The once-sterling reputation of NASA was tarnished, and its bureaucratic ganglia were exposed for all to see.

And we were all taken back to that wretched day seventeen years ago, and reminded that mankind's wings are as fragile as those of Icarus.

ABOUT THE AUTHOR

JACK OHMAN is the editorial cartoonist for *The Oregonian.* He draws, writes, slices, dices, gives speeches, goes fishing and doesn't give his yard the attention it deserves. This is his first book.